FIX YOUR BICYCLE

By
ED SCOTT

ALAN AHLSTRAND
Editor

JEFF ROBINSON
Publisher

CLYMER PUBLICATIONS

*World's largest publisher of books devoted exclusively to
automobiles and motorcycles.*

12860 MUSCATINE STREET · P.O. BOX 4520 · ARLETA, CALIFORNIA 91333-4520

FIRST EDITION
First Printing April, 1972
Second Printing June, 1972
Third Printing May, 1973
Fourth Printing June, 1975

SECOND EDITION
First Printing November, 1975
Second Printing April, 1977
Third Printing June, 1978
Fourth Printing January, 1980
Fifth Printing February, 1982

THIRD EDITION
First Printing January, 1984
Second Printing August, 1984
Third Printing April, 1986
Fourth Printing December, 1986

Printed in U.S.A.

ISBN: 0-89287-035-4

MOTORCYCLE INDUSTRY COUNCIL

Production Coordinator, Victor Williams

*Technical assistance by Neill Evens of I. Martin Imports, Los Angeles, CA and Jerry Bartlett of Laguna
Distributing, Laguna Hills, CA. Technical illustrations by Mitzi McCarthy.*

*COVER: Photographed by Michael Brown Photographic Productions, Los Angeles, California. Assisted by Tim
Lunde. Special thanks to the Marina Del Rey Cycling Club, Marina Del Rey, CA for their patient assistance.*

CONTENTS

FIX YOUR BICYCLE

CHAPTER ONE

GENERAL INFORMATION

Although bicycles have long been a favorite with children, they also play a major role in adult recreation and physical fitness. Today they are more numerous and are being ridden more often than ever before.

In addition to dealers who sell only bicycles, many other retail outlets (toy stores, department stores, discount stores, etc.) also stock them. The number of competent mechanics available cannot keep pace with the demand. Bicycle owners must often do their own maintenance, particularly when on a long tour.

Bicycle repair is not difficult if you know what tools to use and what to do. Anyone not afraid to get their hands dirty, of average intelligence and with some mechanical ability can perform most of the procedures in this book.

In some cases, a repair job may require tools or skills not reasonably expected of the home mechanic. These instances are noted in each chapter and it is recommended that you take the job to your dealer.

This detailed, comprehensive manual covers the majority of the bicycles produced in the world today. The expert text gives complete information on maintenance, repair and replacement of all parts of the bicycle. Hundreds of photos and drawings guide you

through every step. The book includes all you need to keep your bicycle in top shape. **Figure 1** shows a typical bicycle and labels all of the components as they are referred to throughout this manual.

A shop manual is a reference. You want to be able to find information fast. As in all Clymer books, this one is designed with you in mind. All chapters are thumb tabbed. Important items are extensively indexed at the rear of the book. All procedures, tables, photos, etc., in this manual assume that the reader may be working on the bicycle or using this manual for the first time.

Keep the book handy in your tool box. It will help you to better understand how the bicycle operates, lower repair and maintenance costs and generally improve your satisfaction with the bicycle.

WHICH BICYCLES ARE INCLUDED?

At first glance, bicycle manufacturers apparently produce countless different models. But that's not entirely true. Since there are relatively few manufacturers of bicycle *components* (brakes, derailleurs, etc.), all bicycles are remarkably similar. Brakes used by one manufacturer will also be used by many other manufacturers in many different

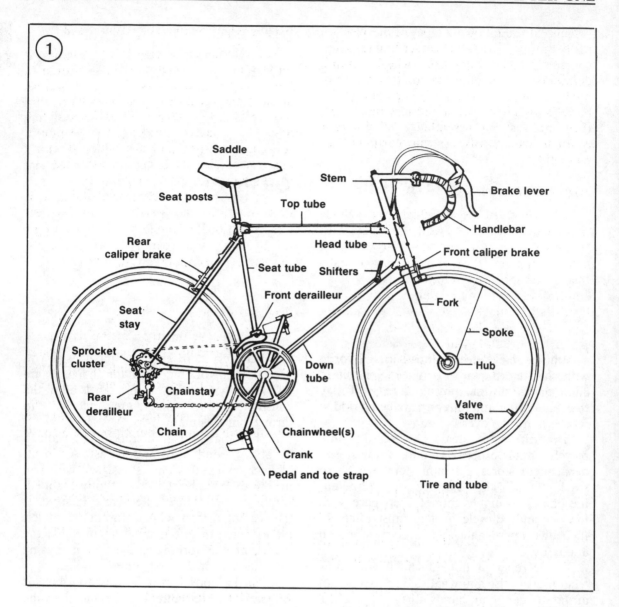

① Saddle, Seat posts, Top tube, Stem, Brake lever, Handlebar, Rear caliper brake, Head tube, Front caliper brake, Seat tube, Shifters, Front derailleur, Fork, Seat stay, Spoke, Sprocket cluster, Down tube, Hub, Rear derailleur, Chainstay, Chain, Chainwheel(s), Valve stem, Crank, Pedal and toe strap, Tire and tube

parts of the world. In addition, different component manufacturers often produce nearly identical items. Service procedures for one brand often work just as well as with others.

TYPES OF BICYCLES

Most types of bicycles in use today are included in this book. Some types are no longer as popular as they have been in the past; others are relatively new and have enjoyed great sales success. Who would have thought a few years ago that today there

would be a bicycle designed specifically for mountain trail riding and for camping? The mountain bicycle is available because it fits a very specific need for certain individuals. This type of bicycle is not completely new, it is just the right combination of components assembled into a unique vehicle.

Within each type of bicycle there are many different variations. These variations relate not only to features but also to price. If you go to a reputable bicycle dealership and explain exactly what you are looking for and how much you want to spend, chances are they will have just the bicycle for you.

None of the following types of bicycles are really unique. The same caliper brakes, same coaster brake, hubs or wheels, same derailleur, etc., may be used on many different bicycle types. Therefore none of the bicycles are either old, brand new or unique; they are just an assemblage of different components to satisfy a specific portion of the marketplace.

High-rise (Juvenile)

This is usually the first 2-wheeled vehicle that a child uses. It is usually equipped with removable training wheels, large-section balloon tires on 20 in. rims, a coaster brake that is easier for a child to use, a large comfortable seat and rubber pedals. The handlebar is either of the raised or high-rise type. These bicycles are heavy-duty to take the abuse of a child learning how to ride.

Some of the more expensive models have either a 3-speed rear hub or a 5-speed rear derailleur. This makes them very maneuverable and they can be used for acrobatic riding.

BMX (Bicycle Moto-cross)

This bicycle is used primarily in BMX racing (a spin-off from motorcycle moto-cross racing). This is where the younger brother and sister can emulate their older brother, sister or parent. Actually, BMX racing is great for kids of all ages. Some BMX racers are in their 20's and still going strong.

BMX bicycles are built with weight reduction, strength and performance in mind. The frame and fork are usually made of chrome-moly steel while the handlebar is either chrome-moly or an aluminum alloy. Braking is accomplished either with a coaster or caliper type hand brake. The lighter and stronger the better for all components; all rotating components must have very low rolling resistance. A lot of money is spent on exotic bearings for the headset, bottom bracket assembly, pedals and hubs. All of the components are made of a lightweight alloy to keep the total vehicle weight to a minimum. The standard rim/tire combination is a 20 in. rim with large-section knobby tires.

Middleweight Single- and Multi-speed

The middleweight bicycle of yesterday is really the heavyweight of today. Some of these weighed as much as 60 lb. (27 kg). Most of these models are either a single-speed with coaster brake or have a 2- or 3-speed hub with a coaster brake. For smooth, comfortable riding they are equipped with a raised handlebar, large spring-cushioned seat and balloon tires on 24 or 26 in. rims.

This type is okay for flat-land riding. It is well suited to industrial use for in-plant transportation and delivery. Because of its weight and lack of gears it is best suited for short rides—definitely not for hills.

Beach Cruisers

Just as the name implies, this is a great bicycle for pedaling around at the beach. Most models have a medium weight frame, but some of the expensive models have a lightweight frame. The cruiser may be fitted with a single-speed and coaster brake, a 3-speed hub with a coaster brake or a 5-speed derailleur with a caliper type hand brake on the rear.

For smooth, comfortable riding they are equipped with a large spring-cushioned seat and balloon tires (1 3/4 in.) on 24 or 26 in. rims. This is definitely not the type of bicycle for a long trip.

Lightweight Multi-speed

These models are equipped with a 5-, 10-, 12- or 18-speed derailleur hub and chainwheels. They have a caliper type hand brake on both the front and rear wheel. The handlebar may be either the raised type or the deep drop type. The deep drop type allows the rider to ride in a lower position for less air drag. For smooth, comfortable riding they are equipped with a mid-sized spring-cushioned seat and narrow-section tires (1 1/4 in.) on 26 or 27 in. rims.

This type is easy to pedal and manuever, is quite comfortable to ride and is good for commuting or recreational riding.

Touring

These models are equipped with a 10-, 12-, 15- or 18-speed derailleur hub and chainwheels. They have a caliper type hand brake on both the front and rear wheel. The handlebar is the deep drop type which allows the rider to ride in a lower position for less air drag. The frame is made of an alloy steel for light weight and strength. The lightweight metal pedals are equipped with toe clips. They can also be disassembled for bearing cleaning and lubrication. All of the components are made of a lightweight alloy to keep the total vehicle weight to a minimum.

The narrow-section tires (1 1/4 in. wide) on 27 in. rims are usually of the clincher type. Some models may be equipped with the sew-up type which have a very low rolling resistance and are glued to a very lightweight rim.

This bicycle is easy to pedal and is very manueverable. It is designed for long rides and hilly terrain. For the serious tourer, racks and pannier bags can be added to both the front and rear wheel.

Road Racing

The road racing bicycle is very similar to the touring bicycle except that all components are of a higher quality and light weight is even more important. Precision quality bearings are used throughout the bicycle and are almost friction-free. This bicycle has a short wheelbase and is very responsive. It is meant to be ridden on smooth flat surfaces.

Mountain Bike

The mountain bicycle is designed specifically for mountain trail riding and for camping use. These models are usually equipped with an 18-speed derailleur hub and chainwheels. They have a cantilever caliper type hand brake on both the front and rear wheel. This type of brake is designed for maximum leverage and brake pressure on the rims. Powerful brakes are necessary on the steep trails that may be encountered.

The handlebar and steering stem is an integral unit on most models. The handlebar is almost straight and is placed well forward for good control on mountain trails. The frame is very rugged and is made of chrome-moly tubing for maximum strength. The metal pedals are lightweight and can be dissassembled for bearing cleaning and lubrication.

All of the components are made of a lightweight alloy to keep the total weight to a minimum. The seat is medium in size and balloon tires (2 1/4 in.) are used on 26 in. rims.

This bike is easy to pedal and is very manueverable. It is designed for long trips in hilly terrain. For the serious mountaineer and camper, racks and pannier bags can be added to both the front and rear.

Tandem Bicycle

The tandem bicycle is the old fashioned "bicycle built for two" (or 3, if the 3rd one is a child). There are as many variations on the tandem bicycle as there are on the ones designed for a single rider. Tandem are built as medium weight single-speeds, lightweight multi-speeds or touring types.

3-wheel Adult Bicycle

These bicycles are often found in retirement communities. The senior citizens use them for transportation, shopping and recreation. There is usually a large basket that fits between the 2 rear wheels. The 3-wheeler may be a single-speed with a coaster brake or have a 3-speed hub with a coaster brake.

For smooth, comfortable riding they are equipped with a very large spring-cushioned seat and balloon tires (1 3/4 in.) on 24 or 26 in. rims.

Folding Bicycle

The folding or collapsible bicycle is a unique little vehicle. It can be folded in half and taken on an airplane, train or bus or can be placed in the trunk of your car. It usually has balloon tires (1 3/4 in.) on 16, 20 or 24 in. rims. Most models are equipped with a 5-speed derailleur hub and chainwheel. They have a caliper type hand brake on both the front and rear wheel. The handlebar is the high rise type for added comfort.

Custom Bicycle

The custom bicycle is one of the most fun, and most expensive, bicycles since you actually build it up out of available components that best suit your specific needs. This type of bicycle is usually an "adult toy" for someone that has just about everything else.

You pick and choose from the many components that are available today—frame, fork, brakes, derailleurs, wheels, tires and handlebar—and there it is, your unique bicycle built to your own specifications.

Be aware of variations of thread configuration and other important details. Be sure to talk this project over with the bicycle dealer to make sure these components are compatible prior to purchasing them. Use the bicycle dealer's knowledge and expertise; they have probably done this many times and know what will and what will not work. A reputable dealer will guide you in the right direction.

MANUAL ORGANIZATION

This manual includes service information for virtually every American, Asian or European bicycle. It is laid out clearly and simply, to aid novices and experts alike.

Chapter Two provides information about basic hand tools. It will help you select the proper tools and use them correctly. In addition, Chapter Two includes basic information about fasteners (screws, nuts, etc.) and useful mechanics' tips.

Chapter Three is probably the most important chapter of the manual. It explains all periodic lubrication and maintenance necessary to keep your bicycle working well and safely.

Chapters Four through Nine provide detailed information and step-by-step procedures for repair or replacement of virtually every part of a bicycle. Each chapter also includes a section describing part-related troubles and how to cure them.

Chapter Ten provides information for assembling a new, crated bicycle. This chapter supplements the manufacturer's instructions which are often poorly written or translated. In addition, this chapter describes how to adjust any bicycle to fit your body dimensions. You can ride at peak efficiency only on a properly adjusted machine.

Chapter Eleven covers clothing and accessories; it will help you pick the right ones to make cycling safer and more enjoyable.

Chapter Twelve takes the mystery out of bicycle gearing. The text describes derailleur-equipped bicycles and those with multi-speed hubs.

Chapter Thirteen tells how to ride a bicycle safely. This chapter is very important for either the first time rider or an older rider who grew up on a heavyweight single or 3-speed bicycle as a child. The newer lightweight bicycles handle very differently; it is a good idea to review this chapter so that you will be able to enjoy your new bicycle to the fullest.

All dimensions and capacities are expressed in English units familiar to U.S. mechanics as well as in metric units.

Some of the procedures in this manual specify special tools. In most cases, the tool is illustrated either in actual use or alone. Well-equipped mechanics may find they can substitute similar tools already on hand or can fabricate their own.

The terms NOTE, CAUTION and WARNING have a specific meaning in this manual. A NOTE provides additional information to make a step or procedure easier or clearer. Disregarding a NOTE could cause inconvenience, but would not cause equipment damage or personal injury.

A CAUTION emphasizes areas where equipment damage could result. Disregarding a CAUTION could cause permanent mechanical damage; however, personal injury is unlikely.

A WARNING emphasizes areas where personal injury or even death could result from negligence. Mechanical damage may also occur. WARNINGS *are to be taken seriously.* In some cases, serious injury or death has resulted from disregarding similar warnings.

Throughout this manual keep in mind 2 conventions. "Front" refers to the front of the bicycle. The front of any component is the end which is installed toward the front of the bicycle. The "left-" and "right-hand" sides refer to the position of the parts as viewed by a rider sitting on the saddle facing forward. For example, the chain wheel and sprocket are on the right-hand side. These rules are simple, but even experienced mechanics occasionally become disoriented.

SERVICE HINTS

Most of the service procedures covered in this manual are straightforward and can be performed by anyone reasonably handy with tools. It is suggested, however, that you consider your own capabilities carefully before attempting any complex operation.

Some tasks require the use of special tools that are not readily available to the public. It may be cheaper to have the job performed by a dealer than to purchase the special equipment and only use it once.

There are many items available that can be used on your hands before and after working on your bicycle. A little preparation prior to getting "all greased up" will help when cleaning up later.

Before starting out, work Vaseline, soap or a product such as Pro-Tek into your hands and under your fingernails and cuticles. This will make cleanup a lot easier.

For cleanup, use a waterless hand soap such as Sta-Lube and then finish up with powdered Boraxo and a fingernail brush.

Repairs go much faster and easier if the bicycle is clean before you begin work. Clean off the surrounding area with a shop cloth and cleaning solvent. Remove all dirt and road grease prior to removing any component.

WARNING
Never use gasoline as a cleaning agent. It presents an extreme fire hazard. Be sure to work in a well-ventilated area when using cleaning solvent. Keep a fire extinguisher, rated for gasoline fires, handy in any case.

Special tools are required for some repair procedures. These may be purchased from a dealer, rented from a tool rental shop or fabricated by a mechanic or machinist (often at a considerable savings).

Much of the labor charged for repairs made by dealers is for the removal and disassembly of other parts to reach the defective unit. It is frequently possible to perform the preliminary operations yourself and then take the defective unit in to the dealer for repair.

Once you have decided to tackle the job yourself, read the entire section in this manual which pertains to it, making sure you have identified the proper section. Study the illustrations and text until you have a good idea of what is involved in completing the job satisfactorily. If special tools are required, make arrangements to get them before you start. It is frustrating and time-consuming to get partly into a job and then be unable to complete it.

During disassembly of parts keep a few general cautions in mind. Force is rarely needed to get things apart. If parts are a tight fit, such as a bearing in a case, there is usually a tool designed to separate them. Never use a screwdriver to pry apart parts with machined surfaces.

Make diagrams (or take a Polaroid picture) wherever similar-appearing parts are found. You may think you can remember where everything came from, but mistakes are costly. There is also the possibility you may be sidetracked and not return to work for days or even weeks, in which interval carefully laid-out parts may have become disturbed.

Tag all similar internal parts for location and mark all mating parts for position. Record number and thickness of any shims as they are removed. Small parts such as bolts can be identified by placing them in plastic sandwich bags. Seal and label them with masking tape.

Protect finished surfaces from physical damage or corrosion.

Frozen or very tight bolts and screws can often be loosened by soaking with penetrating oil, such as WD-40 or Liquid Wrench, then sharply striking the bolt head a few times with a hammer and punch (or screwdriver for screws). Avoid heat unless absolutely necessary, since it may melt, warp or remove the temper from many parts.

No parts, except those assembled with a press fit, require unusual force during assembly. If a part is hard to remove or install, find out why before proceeding.

When assembling 2 parts, start all fasteners, then tighten evenly.

When assembling parts, be sure all shims and washers are installed exactly as they came out.

Whenever a rotating part butts against a stationary part, look for a shim or washer.

Heavy grease can be used to hold small parts in place if they tend to fall out during assembly. However, keep grease and oil away from brake components and electrical accessories.

Take your time and do the job right.

SAFETY FIRST

Professional mechanics can work for years and never sustain a serious injury. If you observe a few rules of common sense and safety, you can enjoy many hours servicing your own bicycle. If you ignore these rules you can hurt yourself or damage the bicycle.
1. Never use gasoline as a cleaning solvent.
2. Never smoke or use a torch in the vicinity of flammable liquids such as cleaning solvent in open containers.
3. Use the proper size wrenches to avoid damage to nuts and injury to yourself.
4. When loosening a tight or stuck nut, think about what would happen if the wrench should slip. Be careful; protect yourself accordingly.
5. Keep your work area clean and uncluttered.
6. Wear safety goggles during all operations involving drilling, grinding or the use of a cold chisel.
7. Never use worn tools.
8. When replacing missing or broken fasteners (bolts, nuts and screws), always use specified replacement parts. They are specially hardened for each application. The wrong 50-cent bolt could easily cause serious and expensive damage, not to mention rider injury.

EXPENDABLE SUPPLIES

Certain expendable supplies are required during maintenance and repair work. These include grease, special oil, wiping rags and cleaning solvent. Ask your dealer for the special lubricants and other products which make bicycle maintenance simpler and easier. Cleaning solvent or kerosene is available at some service stations.

PARTS REPLACEMENT

Small replacement parts for bicycle components are notoriously difficult to find even from a large volume dealer. In many cases the only alternative is to replace the entire assembly. You will often be told in this book to simply remove the defective assembly and replace it with a new assembly. With the large number of bicycles and bicycle components produced throughout the world today, the price of many components has dropped drastically. In many cases it is cheaper and better in the long run to replace the entire derailleur or brake caliper assembly than to try to find the replacement part. Most dealers do not even carry replacement parts for some components. Adding a new part to a worn assembly, such as a derailleur, will make adjustment difficult and tend to cause erratic wear on the new part as well as the remaining old parts.

Whether you are purchasing a spare part or an entire component, always take the old part(s) to the bicycle dealer. The large variety of nearly identical parts makes it difficult to explain exactly what you want. By examining the old part, the dealer will be able to come up with a satisfactory replacement.

CHAPTER TWO

BASIC HAND TOOLS

A number of tools are required to maintain a bicycle in top condition. You may already have some around for other work such as home, motorcycle and car repairs. There are also tools made especially for bicycle repair; you will have to purchase them. In any case, a wide variety of quality tools will make bicycle repairs more effective and convenient. Don't try to buy everything in all sizes in the beginning; buy a little at a time until you have all the necessary tools.

Top quality tools are essential—and also more economical. Poor grade tools are made of inferior materials and are thick, heavy and clumsy. Their rough finish makes them difficult to clean and they usually don't stand up long.

Quality tools are made of alloy steel and are heat treated for greater strength. They are lighter and better balanced than inferior ones. Their surface finish is smooth, making them a pleasure to work with and easy to clean. The initial cost of top quality tools may be relatively high, but longer life and ease of use make them less expensive in the long run.

Keep your tools clean and in a tool box. Keep them organized with sockets and related drives together, open end and box wrenches together, etc. After using a tool, wipe off dirt and grease with a clean cloth and put the tool in its correct place. Doing this will save a lot of time you would have spent trying to find a tool buried in a bunch of spokes and other spare parts.

This chapter describes various hand tools required to perform virtually any repair job on a bicycle. Each tool is described and recommendations as to proper size are made for those not familiar with hand tools. **Table 1** includes tools for emergency repairs on the road. **Table 2** includes tools which should be on hand at home for simple repairs or major overhaul. Tool kits (**Figure 1**) are available from most bicycle shops in a handy carrying pouch.

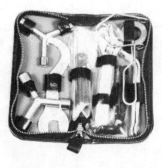

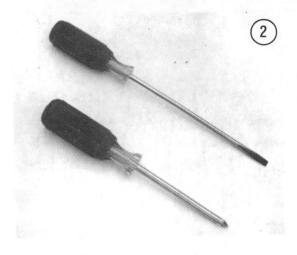

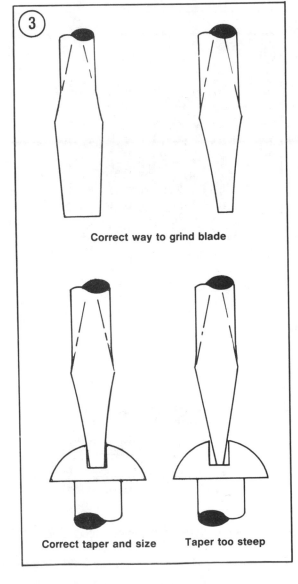

Correct way to grind blade

Correct taper and size   Taper too steep

BASIC HAND TOOLS

Screwdriver

The screwdriver is a very basic tool, but if used improperly it will do more damage than good. The slot on a screw has definite dimensions and shape. A screwdriver must be selected to conform to that shape. Use a small screwdriver for small screws and a large screwdriver for large screws or the screw head will be damaged.

Two basic types of screwdriver are required to repair a bicycle—a common (flat-blade) screwdriver and the Phillips screwdriver (**Figure 2**).

Screwdrivers are available in sets which often include an assortment of common and Phillips blades. If you buy them individually, buy at least the following:

    a. Common screwdriver, 5/16×6 in. blade.

    b. Common screwdriver, 3/8×12 in. blade.

    c. Phillips screwdriver, size 2 tip, 6 in. blade.

Use screwdrivers only for driving screws. Never use a screwdriver for prying or chiseling. In addition, never use a common screwdriver to remove a Phillips or Allen head screw; you can damage the head so that even the proper tool cannot remove the screw.

Keep screwdrivers in proper condition and they will last longer and work better. Always keep the tip in good condition. **Figure 3** shows how to grind the tip to the proper shape if it becomes damaged. Note the parallel sides at the tip.

Pliers

Pliers come in a wide range of types and sizes. Pliers are useful for cutting, bending and crimping. They should never be used to cut hardened objects or to turn nuts or bolts. **Figure 4** shows several pliers useful in bicycle repairs.

Each type of pliers has a specialized function. Gas pliers are general purpose and are used mainly for holding things and for bending. Vise Grips are used as pliers or to

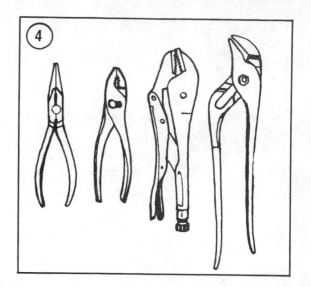

grip objects very tightly like a vise. Needlenose pliers are used to hold or bend small objects. Channel lock pliers can be adjusted to hold various sizes of objects; the jaws remain parallel to grip around objects such as pipe or tubing. There are many more types of pliers. The ones described here are most suitable for bicycle repairs.

Box and Open-end Wrenches

Box wrenches and open-end wrenches are available in sets or separately in a variety of sizes. See **Figure 5** and **Figure 6**. The size stamped near the end refers to the distance between 2 parallel flats on a hex head nut or bolt.

Open end wrenches grip the fastener on only 2 flats. Unless it fits well, it may slip and round off the points on the nut. The box wrench grips all 6 flats. Both 6-point and 12-point openings on box wrenches are available. The 6-point gives superior holding power; the 12-point allows a shorter swing.

Combination wrenches which are open on one end and boxed on the other are also available. Both ends are the same size.

The majority of, *but not all*, bicycles manufactured today require metric wrenches. If in doubt as to which type of tool you will need, check with a bicycle shop. A set covering 7 mm to 19 mm is adequate. Some older American bicycles have English (inch) size hardware. A set covering 1/4 to 3/4 inch is sufficient.

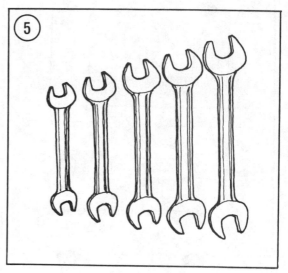

Adjustable (Crescent) Wrenches

An adjustable wrench (also called crescent wrench) can be adjusted to fit nearly any nut or bolt head. See **Figure 7**. However, it can loosen or slip, causing damage to the nut and maybe to your knuckles. Use only when other wrenches are not available.

Crescent wrenches come in sizes ranging from 4-18 in. overall. A 6 or 8 in. size is recommended as an all-purpose wrench.

Socket Wrenches

This type of wrench is undoubtedly the fastest, safest and most convenient to use. See **Figure 8**. Sockets which attach to a ratchet

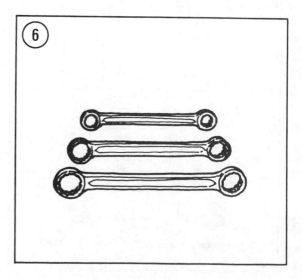

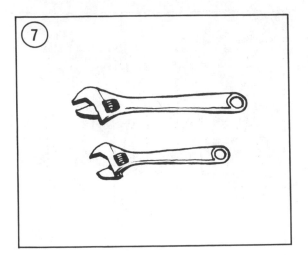

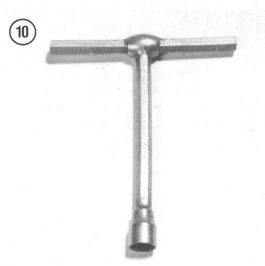

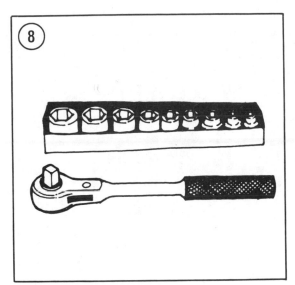

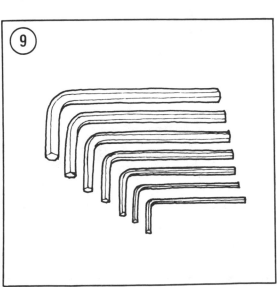

handle are available with 6-point or 12-point openings and 1/4, 3/8, 1/2 and 3/4 inch drives. The drive size indicates the size of the square drive hole which mates with the ratchet handle. Sockets are available in metric and inch sizes.

Socket wrench sets are relatively expensive. For bicycle repairs, it may be wiser to invest in good quality box and open-end wrenches.

Allen Wrenches

These hex-shaped wrenches fit similar shaped recesses in the top of Allen head screws and bolts. See **Figure 9**. For most bicycles 8 mm, 9 mm and 10 mm Allen wrenches are needed. Check the sizes on your bicycle prior to purchasing any Allen wrenches. Special combination Allen and socket wrenches (**Figure 10**) are available from most bicycle shops.

Hammers

The correct hammer is necessary for some bicycle repairs. Use only a hammer with a face (or head) of rubber or plastic or a soft-faced type that is filled with buck shot. Never use a metal-faced hammer on the bicycle; severe damage will result in most cases. You can always produce the same amount of force with a soft-faced hammer.

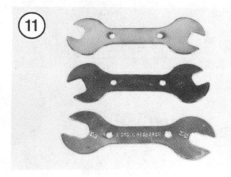

Cone Wrenches

Cone wrenches are nothing more than very thin open-end wrenches (**Figure 11**). These wrenches are available separately or in sets of metric or inch sizes. Obtain the size(s) that fit your bicycle. They are available at most bicycle shops.

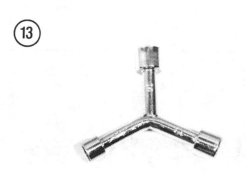

Universal and T-wrenches

Many universal wrenches (**Figure 12** and **Figure 13**) and T-wrenches (**Figure 14**) are available. Before buying one, make sure it actually will fit all the hardware on your bike. If it doesn't, you will still have to carry additional wrenches which defeats the purpose of a universal wrench. Some are of poor quality so choose carefully or, better yet, buy one of the small tool kits made for bikes (**Figure 1**).

Spoke Wrench

These special wrenches (**Figure 15**) are used to tighten spokes. They are available at most bicycle shops.

Cable Cutter

A cable cutter is useful for cutting brake and derailleur cables. Use the type with V-shaped jaws which shear the cable cleanly (**Figure 16**). Wire cutters (which pinch the cable) can be used, but they flatten the ends of the cable making it almost impossible to thread the cable into its housing.

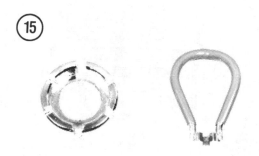

Chain Tool

A chain tool removes rivets from the bicycle chain. **Figure 17** shows a typical design. Chapter Six explains its use.

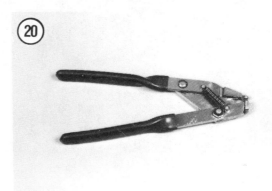

2

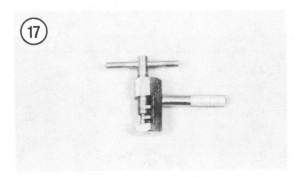

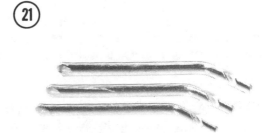

Freewheel Cluster Tool

These tools are used to remove the freewheel cluster on bicycles so equipped, particularly on multi-speed derailleur types. Two basic types are used (**Figure 18**). One type is splined to remove clusters that have internal splines. The other type has prongs to remove clusters without splines. The repair procedures in Chapter Six indicate which type is required for your bicycle.

"Third Hand" and "Fourth Hand" Tools

A special tool such as the Brake Arm Squeezers shown in **Figure 19** and **Figure 20** is very useful for adjusting caliper brakes. These tools act as an additional hand to hold the brake shoes firmly against the wheel rim and, in the case of the "Fourth Hand," to actually pull on the cable. Therefore, both of your hands are free to adjust the cable.

Tire Lever

These are used to remove or install bicycle tires (**Figure 21**). Check the working end of

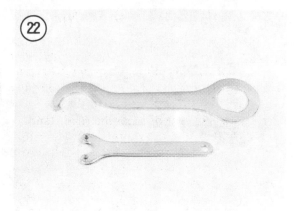

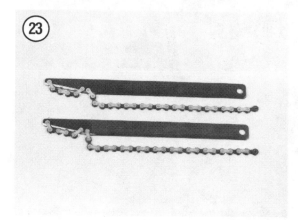

the tool before using the tool and remove any burrs that may damage the inner tube. Never use a screwdriver in place of a tire lever.

Bottom Bracket Tools

These tools are necessary for removal and installation of the bottom bracket assembly. They are also used for adjusting the bottom bracket. **Figure 22** shows a typical set of tools.

Cog (Sprocket) Wrenches

Cog (sprocket) wrenches (**Figure 23**) are necessary to remove the sprockets from the freewheel. Two cog wrenches are required as explained in Chapter Six.

Other Special Tools

Some special tools are required to work on a particular manufacturer's components. Rather than list them all in this chapter, special tools of this type are described with the repair procedure for the component. Also check with a bicycle shop for any additonal tools that may be available.

BICYCLE REPAIR STAND

Most bicycle repairs are easier and quicker if the bicycle is held firmly off the ground. The stand permits you to turn the pedal crank and wheels and operate the shift mechanism. Commercially built repair stands are available or you can fabricate one of your own (**Figure 24**) for home repair use.

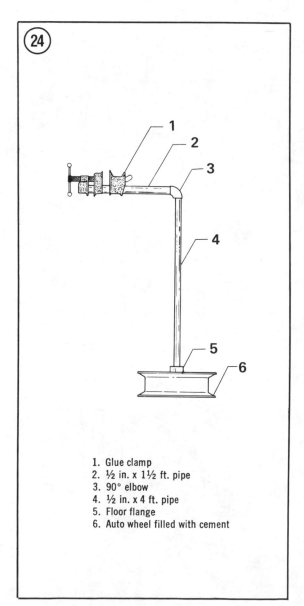

1. Glue clamp
2. ½ in. x 1½ ft. pipe
3. 90° elbow
4. ½ in. x 4 ft. pipe
5. Floor flange
6. Auto wheel filled with cement

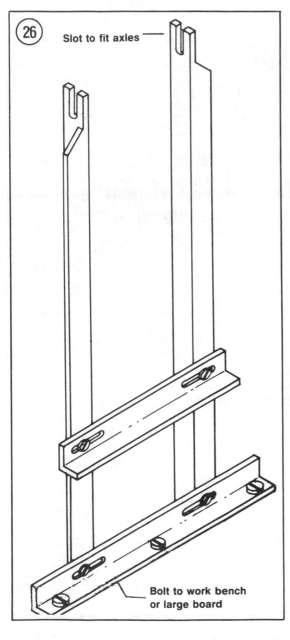

Slot to fit axles

Bolt to work bench
or large board

WHEEL TRUING STAND

If you plan to lace your own wheels or keep your present wheels properly aligned, you must have a truing stand. Commercial stands are available (**Figure 25**) but some are quite expensive. You can build your own for a fraction of the cost of a commercial stand.

Figure 26 shows an easy-to-construct stand. None of the dimensions are critical. There must be enough clearance between the axle slots and the top brace to fit the largest wheel you anticipate—usually about 14 in. (551 mm) to clear a 27 in. wheel easily. The distance between upright pieces must be adjustable from the smallest to the largest axle lengths anticipated. Most front axles are 3.66-3.94 in. (93-100 mm) and most rear axles are 4.02-5.00 in. (102-127.6 mm) in length. Some tandems may be as wide as 5.51 in. (140 mm).

To use the stand, loosen the screws in the slots and adjust the width of the stand to fit the wheel. Mount the wheel in the slots with same hardware used to mount the wheel to the frame. If measuring side-to-side wobble, mount a piece of chalk or grease pencil to one of the upright pieces with a C-clamp. To measure out-of-round, clamp the chalk to the top cross brace. Refer to Chapter Four for specific instructions for truing (aligning) wheels.

FASTENERS

To better understand and select basic hand tools, a knowledge of various fasteners used on bicycles is important. This knowledge will also aid in selecting replacements when fasteners are damaged or corroded beyond use.

Threads

Nuts, bolts and screws are manufactured in a wide range of thread patterns. To join a nut and bolt, it is necessary that the diameter of the bolt and the diameter of the hole in the nut be the same. It is equally important that the threads on both be properly matched.

The best way to ensure that threads on 2 fasteners are compatible is to turn the nut on the bolt with your fingers only. If much force is required, check the thread condition on both fasteners. If the thread condition is good but the fasteners jam, the threads are not compatible. Take the fasteners to a hardware store or bicycle dealer for proper mates.

These 3 specifications describe every thread:

a. Diameter.
b. Threads-per-inch (TPI).
c. Thread direction (right-hand or left-hand thread).

Figure 27 shows the first 2 specifications. Several thread patterns that are in common use are:

a. Metric standard.
b. British standards (BSF, BSW and CEI).
c. American standard.
d. Italian standard.

The threads are cut differently as shown in **Figure 28**. The country of manufacture is not a reliable indication of the thread standard used. In fact, manufacturers may mix 2 or more standards on one bicycle. French bicycles exported to the U.S. usually have British thread freewheels. Japanese manufacturers often mix metric standard with American or British standard components on bicycles exported to the U.S.

Most threads are cut so that a fastener must be turned clockwise to tighten it. These are called right-hand threads. Some bicycle components, such a pedals, have left-hand threads; these must be turned counterclockwise to tighten.

When replacing threaded components, rely on your dealer's experience; take the old part in for a replacement.

Machine Screws

There are many different types of machine screws. **Figure 29** shows screw heads requiring different types of turning tools. Heads are designed to protrude above the metal (round) or to be slightly recessed in the metal (flat).

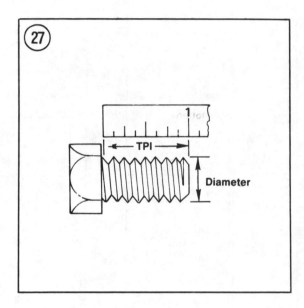

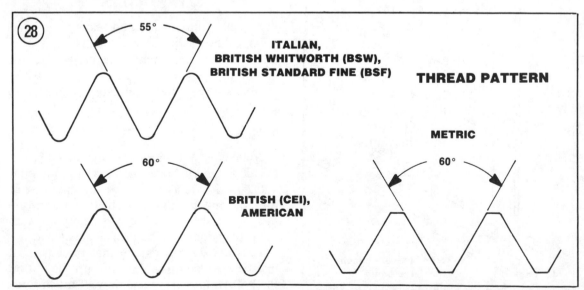

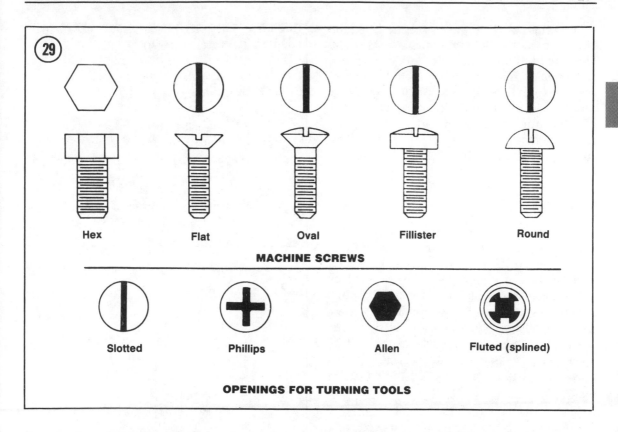

Hex Flat Oval Fillister Round

MACHINE SCREWS

Slotted Phillips Allen Fluted (splined)

OPENINGS FOR TURNING TOOLS

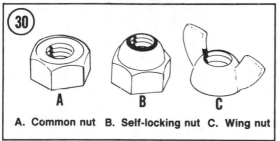

A. Common nut B. Self-locking nut C. Wing nut

When replacing a damaged screw, take it to a hardware store or bicycle shop. Match the head type, diameter and threads exactly. In addition, match the type of metal used. For example, if the old screw is chrome plated, the new one must also be chrome plated to resist corrosion and rust.

Bolts

Commonly called bolts, the technical name for these fasteners is cap screw. They are normally specified by diameter, threads-per-inch (TPI) and length. For example, 1/4-20×1 specifies a bolt 1/4 in. in diameter with 20 TPI by 1 in. long. The measurement across 2 flats on the head of the bolt indicates the proper wrench size to be used.

When replacing damaged bolts, follow the same advice given for machine screws.

Nuts

Nuts are manufactured in a variety of types and sizes. Most nuts on bicycles are hexagonal (6-sided) and fit on bolts, screws and studs with the same diameter and threads-per-inch.

Figure 30 shows several nuts usually found on bicycles. The common nut (A) is normally used with a lockwasher. The self-locking nut (B) has a nylon insert which prevents the nut from loosening and does not require a locknut. To indicate the size of a nut, manufacturers specify the diameter of the opening and the threads-per-inch (TPI). For example, 1/4-20 indicates a 1/4 in. opening and 20 TPI. This is the same as for bolts but with no length dimension given. The measurement across 2 flats on the nut indicates the proper wrench size to be used.

The wing nut (C, **Figure 30**) is designed for fast removal by hand without special tools. They are used on some older model so-called quick-release hubs.

When replacing a damaged nut, take it to a hardware store or bicycle shop. Match the type, diameter and threads exactly. In addition, match the type of metal used (for instance, chrome plating to resist rust and corrosion).

Washers

There are 2 major types of washer—flat washers and lockwashers. Flat washers are simple discs with a hole to fit a screw or bolt. Lockwashers are designed to prevent a fastener from working loose due to vibration, expansion and contraction. **Figure 31** shows several washers. Note that flat washers are often used between a lockwasher and a fastener to act as a smooth bearing surface. This permits the fastener to be turned easily with a tool.

MECHANIC'S TIPS

Removing Frozen Fasteners

When a fastener rusts and cannot be removed, several methods may be used to loosen it. First apply penetrating oil such as Liquid Wrench or WD-40 (available at any hardware store or auto supply store). Apply it liberally and let it stand for 10-15 minutes. Rap the fastener several times with a small hammer; do not hit it hard enough to cause damage. Reapply the penetrating oil if necessary.

For frozen screws, apply oil as described, then insert a screwdriver in the slot and rap the top of the screwdriver with a hammer. This loosens the rust so the screw can be removed in the normal way. If the screw head is too chewed up to use a screwdriver, grip the head with Vise Grip pliers and twist the screw out.

For a frozen bolt or nut, apply penetrating oil, then rap on it with a hammer. Twist off with the proper size wrench. If the points are rounded off, grip with Vise Grip pliers.

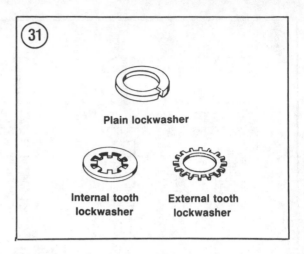

Plain lockwasher

Internal tooth lockwasher

External tooth lockwasher

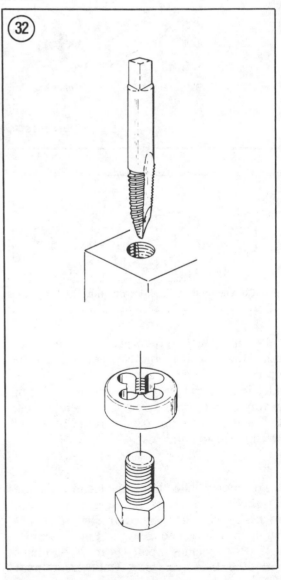

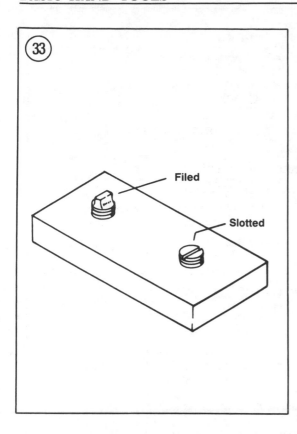

Filed

Slotted

Remedying Stripped Threads

Occasionally, threads are stripped through carelessness or impact damage. Often the threads can be cleaned up by running a tap (for internal threads on nuts) or die (for external threads on bolts) through the threads as shown in **Figure 32**.

Removing Broken Screws or Bolts

When the head breaks off a screw or bolt, several methods are available for removing the remaining portion.

If a large portion of the remainder projects out, try gripping it with Vise Grips. If the projecting portion is too small, file it to fit a wrench or cut a slot in it to fit a screwdriver. See **Figure 33**.

If the head breaks off flush, use a screw extractor. To do this, centerpunch the remaining portion of the screw or bolt. Drill a small hole in the screw and tap the extractor into the hole. Back the screw out with a wrench on the extractor as shown in **Figure 34**.

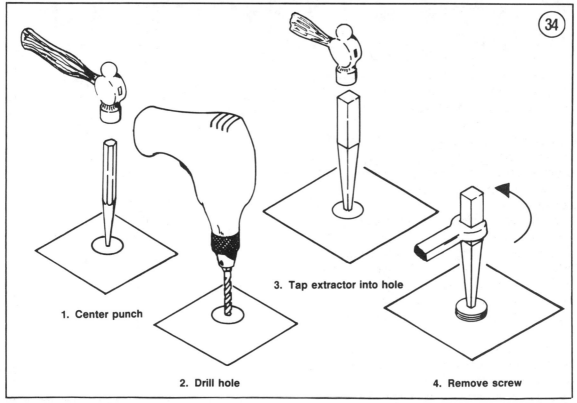

1. Center punch

2. Drill hole

3. Tap extractor into hole

4. Remove screw

Table 1 EMERGENCY TOOL KIT

Tool	Size or specification
Common screwdriver	Choose smallest tools possible to fit
Phillip screwdriver	into small carry pouch.
Cone wrenches	
Crescent wrench	

Table 2 HOME WORKSHOP TOOLS

Tool	Size or specification
Screwdrivers	
Common	5/16×8 in. blade
Common	3/8×12 in. blade
Phillips	Size 2 tip, 6 in. blade
Pliers	
Gas pliers	6 in. overall
Vise Grips	10 in. overall
Needle nose	6 in. overall
Channel lock	12 in. overall
Wrenches	
Box-end set	5/16-3/4 in.[1], 8-19 mm[2]
Open-end set	5/16-3/4 in.[1], 8-19 mm[2]
Crescent (adjustable)	6-8 in. overall
Socket set	3/8 in. drive ratchet with 5/16-3/4 in.[1] or 8-19 mm[2] sockets
Allen set	2-10 mm
Cone wrenches	To fit your bicycle
Spoke wrench	–
Other special tools	
Cable cutter	V-shaped cutting jaws
Chain tool	–
Freewheel cluster tool	Splined or prongs to fit bicycle
Third hand	Weinmann 777 or equivalent
Tire levers	For bicycle tires only

1. American bicycles except derailleur-equipped.
2. American derailleur-equipped and all European and Asian bicycles.

CHAPTER THREE

LUBRICATION AND MAINTENANCE

A bicycle in poor condition is difficult and possibly even unsafe to ride. The chain may slip off, the derailleurs won't shift, the brakes won't stop it and it's hard to pedal. The bicycle rattles and shakes as if it's coming apart. In fact, all these symptoms indicate that it *is* coming apart and needs help.

A bicycle is a relatively expensive and complex machine. Like any precision device, it requires periodic attention to keep it working properly. Without proper attention, the owner will soon face a number of expensive repairs.

Most expensive bicycle repairs are preventable. A regular program of periodic inspection, lubrication and maintenance will help find trouble before it becomes major. These routines will help prevent most troubles due to wear.

This chapter explains periodic adjustments, maintenance, inspection and lubrication required for the bicycle. **Table 1** summarizes this information for quick reference.

You can perform the entire yearly procedure in less than one day. Monthly maintenance for a typical multi-speed takes less than one hour. Considering the number of carefree, safe and enjoyable hours of cycling made possible by a well-maintained bicycle, maintenance time represents a "bargain" investment.

Monthly maintenance should be performed while the bicycle is in continuous use. If it is stored for the winter, monthly maintenance obviously is not necessary. If you cycle more than the average person or ride on rough or dusty roads, perform monthly procedures more often.

Yearly maintenance should be performed just before the major cycling season begins in your area. In most areas, early spring is a good time for this. At the same time, perform maintenance required every 6 months. Six months later perform the 6-month maintenance again, even if you are going to store the bicycle for the winter.

LUBRICANTS
Oil

Oil is graded according to its viscosity, which is an indication of how thick it is. The Society of Automotive Engineers (SAE) system distinguishes oil viscosity by numbers. Thick oils have higher viscosity numbers than thin oils. For example, an SAE 5 oil is thin oil while an SAE 90 oil is relatively thick. The viscosity of an oil has nothing to do with its lubrication properties.

In this manual, many procedures specify light oil. This means an SAE 5 oil or equivalent, such as Schwinn Cycle Oil. A good all-around lubricant is Trifilon, which comes in a spray can.

NOTE
Stay away from 3-in-1 Oil and other vegetable based oils as they tend to gum up with time.

Grease

A good quality grease (preferably waterproof) should be used. Water does not wash grease off parts as easily as it washes off oil. In addition, grease maintains its lubricating qualities better than oil on long hard rides. In a pinch, though, the wrong lubricant is better than none at all. Correct the situation as soon as possible.

A number of procedures in this manual specify thin grease. Lubriplate, a white grease, is highly satisfactory for bicycles and comes in a small tube for easy application. Molybdenum disulfide grease has unique lubricating capabilities and should be used where indicated.

Cleaning Solvents

A number of solvents can be used to remove old dirt, grease and oil. Kerosene is comparatively inexpensive and is available at some service stations. Another inexpensive solvent similar to kerosene is ordinary diesel fuel. Both of these solvents have a very high flash point and can be used safely in any adequately ventilated area away from open flames (including the pilot light on gas appliances which may be in the garage).

WARNING
Never use gasoline as a cleaning agent. It presents an extreme fire hazard. Be sure to work in a well-ventilated area when using cleaning solvent. Keep a fire extinguisher, rated for gasoline fires, handy in any case.

PERIODIC LUBRICATION

Front Wheel Hub

If the hub has an oil fitting, add about 1/2 teaspoon of SAE 20 oil every month. Every 6 months, disassemble, clean, inspect, lubricate and reassemble the hub. Refer to Chapter Six for the correct procedure.

Rear Wheel Hub

On all multi-speed rear hubs or those with a coaster brake, add one tablespoon of oil every month, if the hub has an oil fitting (**Figure 1**). On freewheel rear hubs, once a year completely disassemble, clean, inspect and lubricate the rear hub as described in Chapter Six. Because multi-speed hubs and hubs with coaster brakes are very complex, this procedure is best left to a bicycle dealer.

Chain Cleaning, Inspection and Lubrication

Every month, or more frequently if used in dusty or muddy terrain, remove, thoroughly clean and lubricate the chain.

The chain is one of the most severely stressed parts of the bicycle, yet it is often neglected. Failure to clean the chain regularly will result in premature chain wear. Refer to **Figure 2** for this procedure.

1. Remove the chain as described in Chapter Six or Chapter Seven.
2. Immerse the chain in a pan of cleaning solvent and allow it to soak for about half an hour. Move it around and flex it during this period so that the dirt between the pins and rollers may work its way out.
3. Scrub the rollers and side plates with a stiff toothbrush and rinse away loosened grit.

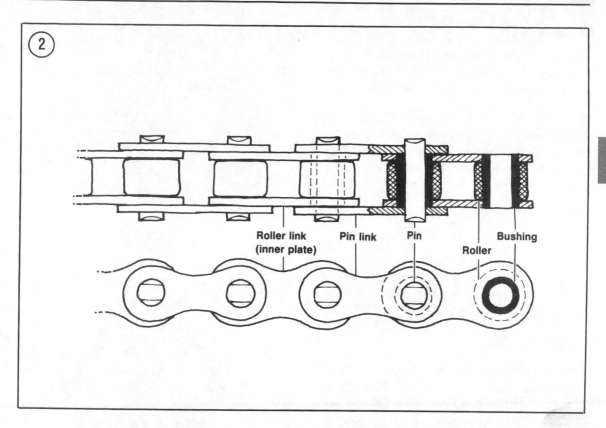

Roller link (inner plate)   Pin link   Pin   Roller   Bushing

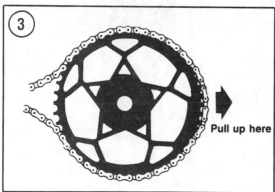

Pull up here

Rinse it a couple of times to make sure all the dirt and grit is washed out. Hang the chain up and allow it to thoroughly dry.

4. After cleaning the chain, examine it carefully for wear or damage. Check that each link is flexible without binding, yet not too loose.

5. Check the inner faces of the inner plates. They should be lightly polished on both sides. If they show considerable wear on both sides the sprocket(s), chainwheel or derailleur may not be aligned properly.

6. Wrap the chain around the chainwheel (front sprocket) as shown in **Figure 3**. Pull on the chain at the point indicated. If it can be pulled away from the chainwheel, it has stretched and must be replaced.

7. Whenever the chain is removed for cleaning and inspection always check the chainwheel and the rear sprocket. Check for bent, worn or missing teeth. Never install a new chain over a worn chainwheel or sprocket.

8. Thoroughly lubricate the chain with SAE 10W motor oil. After the chain is reinstalled on the bicycle, wipe off any excess oil; otherwise, it will fling off onto other parts of the bicycle and your clothes.

9. Install the chain as described in Chapter Six or Chapter Seven.

10. Adjust the tension as described in Chapter Six or Chapter Seven.

Headset (Fork Bearings)

Every 6 months, disassemble the headset. Clean all parts, inspect them and lubricate the bearings as described in Chapter Eight.

Bottom Bracket

Once a year, remove bottom bracket bearings. Clean, inspect and lubricate the crank assembly. Refer to Chapter Six.

Cables

Every month, squirt a few drops of light oil on brake and gear change cables where they enter the cable housing (**Figure 4**).

Brake Calipers

Every month, squirt a few drops of light oil on the brake pivot bolts (**Figure 5**).

> *CAUTION*
> *Do not get oil on the rubber brake pads or tires. Oil on the brake pads will render them useless. Oil causes rubber to deteriorate and can ruin your tires.*

Derailleurs

Every month, squirt a few drops of light oil on moving parts of front (**Figure 6**) and rear (**Figure 7**) derailleurs. Don't forget the jockey and idler wheels (**Figure 8**) on the rear derailleur. Also oil the shifters (**Figure 9**).

Freewheels

On derailleur equipped bicycles, squirt a few drops of light oil into the freewheel mechanism (**Figure 10**) every month.

> *CAUTION*
> *Do not use any oil thicker than SAE 5.*

Every 6 months, remove the freewheel (see Chapter Six), clean it in kerosene and lubricate it.

Pedals

To lubricate pedals, squirt a few drops of SAE 30W oil into each end every month (**Figure 11**).

Every 6 months, disassemble, clean and repack pedals as described in Chapter Six.

PERIODIC ADJUSTMENTS

The following adjustments should be performed at least as often as indicated and more often if the bicycle receives heavy use.

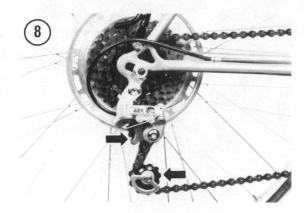

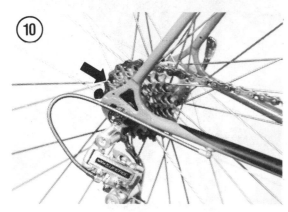

Adjustments required depend on the type of bicycle you have. On single-speed bikes with a coaster brake, there are no periodic adjustments. On bicycles with multi-speed hubs, adjust the caliper (hand) brakes and the front and/or rear derailleur.

Coaster Brake Adjustment

There are no periodic adjustments required on any coaster brake. Make sure that the screw and nut (**Figure 12**) securing the end of the brake arm to the chain stay are tight.

Caliper (Hand) Brake Adjustment

Adjustment of side pull and center pull brakes are identical. The brake shoes are secured to the caliper arms by a nut on each shoe.

For maximum braking efficiency, the shoes must fully contact the rim when engaged, *not the tire*.

NOTE
The wheel must run true in order to properly adjust the caliper brakes.

1. Check each wheel for alignment. Adjust if necessary as described in Chapter Four.
2. Align the brake shoes to the rim as follows:
   a. Loosen the self-locking nut on each shoe and align the brake shoe horizontally with the center of the rim as shown in

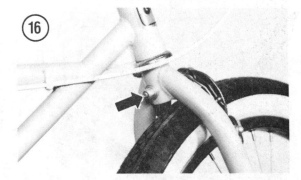

Figure 13. The shoes must fully contact the rim when engaged, *not a portion of the tire* as shown in **Figure 14** and **Figure 15.**

> *WARNING*
> *If the shoe comes in contact with the tire it will quickly wear through, causing a blowout. This could result in a serious accident.*

    b. Tighten the self-locking nut.
    c. Repeat for all 4 shoes.
3. Make sure that both brake shoes on a wheel are the same distance from the rim. If they are not, perform the following:
    a. Loosen the caliper mounting nut (**Figure 16**) or Allen bolt (**Figure 17**) and center the shoes.
    b. Tighten the mounting nut or Allen bolt.
4. Each brake shoe should be 1/16-1/8 in. (1.6-3.2 mm) from the wheel rim when the hand lever is released. If the shoes are the same distance from the rim but closer or farther than specified, perform the following:
    a. Turn the adjusting barrel (A, **Figure 18**) until the shoes are correctly spaced.

b. If the shoes are so far out that you cannot adjust them with the barrel, loosen the cable anchor bolt (B, **Figure 18**).

c. Attach a "Fourth Hand" to the cable (**Figure 19**). Hold the shoes 1/8 in. (3.2 mm) away from the rim, take up the slack in the cable and tighten the cable anchor bolt.

5. To keep the brakes from squeaking, the front of the brake shoe must be 1/32 in. (0.79 mm) closer to the rim than the rear of the shoe. If adjustment is needed, put a wrench on the brake arm directly below the brake shoe assembly and apply a small amount of force to slightly bend the arm.

Cantilever Brake Adjustment

The brake shoes are secured to the caliper arms by an eye bolt, lockwasher and nut. For maximum braking efficiency the shoes must fully contact the rim when engaged, *not the tire.*

NOTE
The wheel must run true in order to properly adjust the caliper brakes.

1. Check each wheel for alignment. Adjust if necessary as described in Chapter Four.

2. Align the brake shoes horizontally to the rim as follows:

a. Loosen the nut (**Figure 20**) on each eye bolt and align the brake shoe horizontally with the center of the rim as shown in **Figure 21**. The shoes must fully contact the rim when engaged, *not a portion of the tire.*

WARNING
If the shoe comes in contact with the tire it will quickly wear through, causing a blowout. This could result in a serious accident.

b. Hold the brake shoe assembly securely and tighten the nut. Do not allow the brake shoe assembly to move while tightening the nut.

c. Repeat for all 4 shoes.

3. Align the brake shoes vertically to the rim as follows:

a. Loosen the nut (**Figure 22**) on each eye bolt and rotate the pivot bolt and the

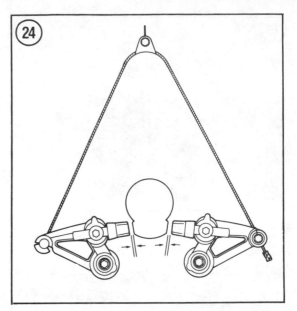

brake shoe vertically so that the shoe will meet the rim squarely when it is applied (**Figure 23**). The shoes must fully contact the rim when engaged, *not a portion of the tire.*

WARNING
If the shoe comes in contact with the tire it will quickly wear through, causing a blowout. This could result in a serious accident.

   b. Hold the brake shoe assembly securedy and tighten the nut. Do not allow the brake shoe assembly to move while tightening the nut.
   c. Repeat for all 4 shoes.

4. Make sure that both brake shoes on a wheel are the same distance from the rim. There must be a *total* clearance of 1/8-5/32 in. (0.32-0.40 mm) from the wheel rim when the hand lever is released (**Figure 24**). If adjustment is necessary, perform the following:
   a. Loosen the nut (**Figure 22**) on each eye bolt and move the brake shoe in or out to the correct dimension. Also make sure that it is aligned horizontally with the center of the rim as shown in **Figure 21**. The shoes must fully contact the rim when engaged.
   b. Hold the brake shoe assembly securely and tighten the nut. Do not allow the brake shoe assembly to move while tightening the nut.
   c. Repeat for all 4 shoes.

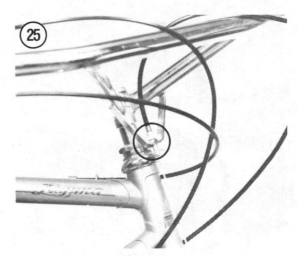

5. If the shoes are so far away that you cannot adjust them on their arms, loosen the cable locknut and turn the adjusting barrel (**Figure 25**) to take up cable slack. Repeat Step 4 for fine adjustment.

6. To keep the brakes from squeaking, the front of the brake shoe must be about 0.02 in. (0.5 mm) closer to the rim than the rear of the shoe (**Figure 26**). If adjustment is needed, perform the following:
   a. Loosen the nut on each eye bolt.
   b. Rotate the eccentric angular washer on the eye bolt to the rod on the brake shoe assembly.
   c. Tighten the nut.

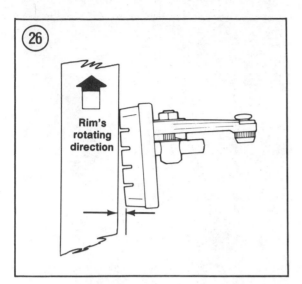

3

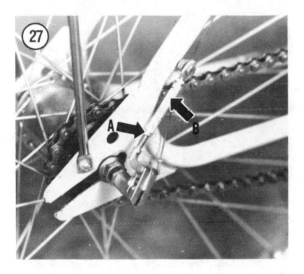

gear without pedal slippage. Readjust the adjusting sleeve, if necessary.

Front Derailleur Adjustment

There are 2 types of front derailleur. Newer models have 2 adjustment screws, while older models have only one adjustment screw. Before adjusting either type, make sure that the derailleur is properly positioned as described under *Front Derailleur Removal/Installation* in Chapter Six.

2 adjustment screws

1. Mount the bicycle in a repair stand or have someone hold the rear wheel off the ground.

CAUTION
Shift gears only while the rear wheel and pedals are in motion or the derailleur may be damaged.

2. To adjust the low side, perform the following:
   a. Rotate the pedals in a forward direction and move the front derailleur shifter all the way to the front. This will shift the chain onto the small front sprocket of the chainwheel.
   b. Rotate the pedals in a forward direction and move the rear derailleur shifter all the way to the rear. This will shift the chain onto the large sprocket of the rear freewheel.

Multi-speed Hub Adjustment

Adjustment is confined to varying cable length with the adjusting sleeve.
1. Mount the bicycle in a repair stand or have someone hold the rear wheel off the ground.
2. Shift the changer into high gear.
3. Loosen the locknut (A, **Figure 27**) and rotate the sleeve (B, **Figure 27**) until cable is just barely slack. Tighten the locknut.
4. Make sure that the cable ferrule clamping screw (**Figure 28**) on the frame is tight. If this clamp is loose it may allow the gears to slip. Tighten if necessary.
5. Shift the changer into second gear. Test ride to ensure that the hub goes into second

c. Make sure that the front derailleur shifter is all the way *forward* and that the cable is *almost* taut.

d. Turn the low gear adjust screw until there is minimal clearance (1/32 in.; 0.8 mm) between the chain and the inside surface of the chain guide (side closest to the frame seat tube). Refer to "L" in **Figures 29-31**.

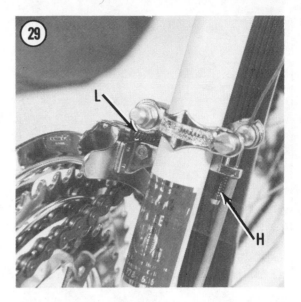

> *NOTE*
> *There must be enough clearance so that the chain does not touch the chain guide.*

> *CAUTION*
> *Shift gears only while rear wheel and pedals are in motion or the derailleur may be damaged.*

3. To adjust the high side, perform the following:

a. Rotate the pedals in a forward direction and move the front derailleur shifter all the way to the rear. This will shift the chain onto the large front sprocket of the chainwheel.

b. Rotate the pedals in a forward direction and move the rear derailleur shifter all the way to the front. This will shift the chain onto the small sprocket of the rear freewheel.

c. Make sure that the front derailleur shifter is all the way *to the rear* and that the cable is *almost* taut.

d. Turn the high gear adjust screw until there is minimal clearance between the chain and the outside surface of the chain guide (side away from the frame seat tube). Refer to "H" in **Figures 29-31**.

> *NOTE*
> *There must be enough clearance so that the chain does not touch the chain guide.*

One adjustment screw

1. Mount the bicycle in a repair stand or have someone hold the rear wheel off the ground.

> *CAUTION*
> *Shift gears only while the rear wheel and pedals are in motion or the derailleur may be damaged.*

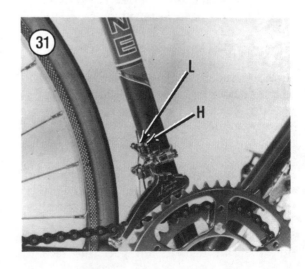

2. Rotate the pedals in a forward direction and move the front derailleur shifter all the way to the front. This will shift the chain onto the small front sprocket of the chainwheel.

3. Rotate the pedals in a forward direction and move the rear derailleur shifter toward the middle of its stroke. This will shift the chain onto the middle gear of the rear freewheel.

4. Make sure that the front derailleur shifter is all the way *forward* and that the cable is *almost taut.*

5. Loosen the bolt holding the chain guide to the spindle (A, **Figure 32**). Move the cage on the spindle until the chain is centered in the cage. Make sure that the curve of the cage is parallel to the curve of the sprocket and tighten the bolt to hold the cage on the spindle.

NOTE
There must be enough clearance so that the chain does not touch the chain guide.

6. Rotate the pedals in a forward direction and move the front derailleur shifter all the

way to the rear. This will shift the chain onto the large front sprocket of the chainwheel.

7. Make sure that the front derailleur shifter is all the way *toward the rear* and that the cable is *almost* taut.

8. Turn the adjust screw (B, **Figure 32**) until the chain guide is centered over the large sprocket.

NOTE
There must be sufficient clearance so that the chain does not touch the chain guide.

9. Rotate the pedals in a forward direction to make sure that the chain does not rub on the cage. Repeat Step 8 if necessary to stop rubbing.

Rear Derailleur Adjustment

There are 2 general types of rear derailleur but adjustment is the same for both types.

1. Mount the bicycle in a repair stand or have someone hold the rear wheel off the ground.

CAUTION
Shift gears only while the rear wheel and pedals are in motion or the derailleur may be damaged.

2. Rotate the pedals in a forward direction and move the front derailleur shifter all the way to the rear. This will shift the chain onto the large front sprocket of the chainwheel.

3. Rotate the pedals in a forward direction and move the rear derailleur shifter all the way to the front. This will shift the chain onto the small sprocket of the rear freewheel.

4. Make sure that the rear derailleur shifter is all the way *forward* and that the cable has a very slight amount of slack.

5. If there is not enough slack, loosen cable anchor bolt (**Figure 33**) on the rear derailleur

and pull cable end until the cable is barely slack. Tighten cable anchor bolt.

6. Turn the high gear adjust screw until the jockey roller (upper roller) is aligned with the centerline of the chain and small sprocket. Refer to "1" in **Figures 34-38**.

7. Rotate the pedals in a forward direction and move the rear derailleur shifter all the way to the rear. This will shift the chain onto the large sprocket of the rear freewheel.

8. Make sure that the rear derailleur shifter is all the way *to the rear* and that the cable has a very slight amount of slack.

9. Turn the low gear adjust screw until the jockey roller (upper roller) is aligned with the centerline of the chain and large sprocket. Refer to "2" in **Figures 34-38**.

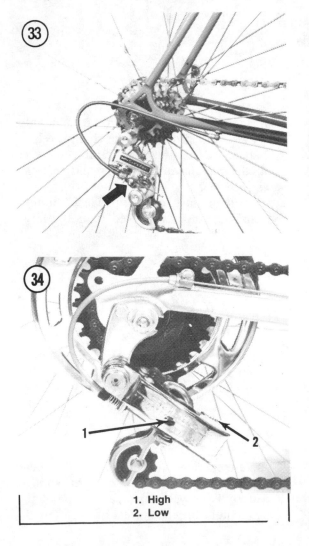

1. High
2. Low

1. High
2. Low

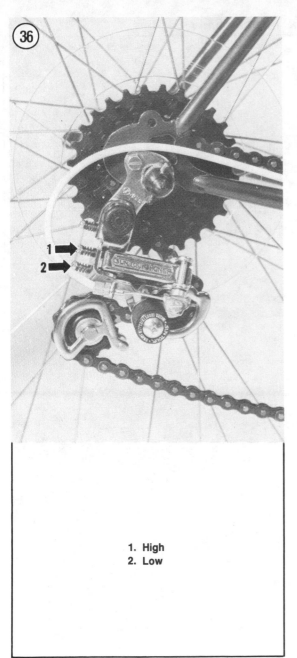

1. High
2. Low

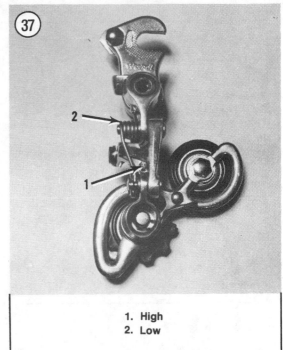

1. High
2. Low

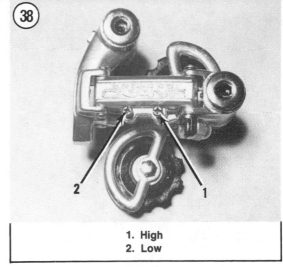

1. High
2. Low

3

Table 1 MAINTENANCE SUMMARY

	Lubricate with oil	Overhaul with grease	Check and/or adjust
Monthly			
Pedals	X		
Freewheel	X		
Derailleurs	X		X
Front & rear hubs	X		
Chain	X		
Cables	X		
Brake calipers	X		X
Every 6 months			
Front hubs		X	
Head set		X	
Freewheel		X	
Pedals		X	
Every year			
Rear hub		X	
Crankset		X	

CHAPTER FOUR

TIRES, TUBES AND WHEELS

Tires, tubes and wheels are vulnerable to damage from any number of objects found on streets, roads and paths. Common sense and care can prevent most of this trouble. Preventive maintenance also cuts down on the frequency of repair.

Table 1 and **Table 2** are located at the end of this chapter.

DESCRIPTION

Tire and Tube Types

There are two types of tire and tube; wired or clincher tires are being used on most bicycles. High performance racing/touring bicycles and track bikes usually have tubular or sew-up tires.

Clincher tires are U-shaped in cross section and are similar to an automobile or motorcycle tire. They are made up of multiple layers of rubber and fabric and must be mounted on a clincher type wheel (**Figure 1**). This type of tire is stronger and heavier than tubular tires and is best suited for bicycles that are subject to many different roadway surfaces. Clincher tires come in a wide range of sizes from large heavy balloon tires to the narrow lightweight tires found on many multi-speed derailleur equipped bicycles.

Tubular tires and wheels (**Figure 2**) can be fitted to any bicycle but they are usually used on touring and racing type derailleur-equipped bicycles. Tubular tires are used mainly for track and road racing or other

situations which call for high performance. These tires range from lightweight (4 oz.) smooth tread designs for track racing to heavier (15-17 oz.) models with specialized treads.

Tubular tires have tubes sewn inside them; some can be folded and stored under the saddle for emergencies. They can easily be replaced if necessary.

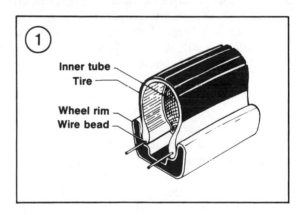

Inner tube
Tire
Wheel rim
Wire bead

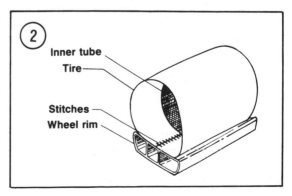

Inner tube
Tire
Stitches
Wheel rim

Tire Valves

Two types of tire valve are used on bicycle tires. The Schraeder type (**Figure 3**) is used on clincher tubes only. Presta valves (**Figure 4**) are used on both clincher and tubular types. Presta valves require a special adaptor for inflation with a bicycle pump.

Tire Inflation

An improperly inflated tire can increase both pedaling effort and tire wear. Due to the small volume of the tube, they should be inflated only with a hand operated air pump. Do not use compressed air such as is available at service stations. Air pressure available at service stations is much greater than that needed in lightweight tires. When air at 150 psi enters a tube through a standard valve core, the pressure increases so rapidly that the tube blows out before you can pull the hose off the stem.

You can minimize blowouts from over-inflation by purchasing a hand pump which can be attached to the bicycle frame or a larger, more efficient hand pump for home use. Test the pump before purchasing it. There are a number of cheaply made ones and also some excellent types (**Figure 5**). Refer to Chapter Eleven for some tips on buying a tire pump.

Table 1 and **Table 2** show recommended inflation pressure for most popular tires. If yours is not included, ask your dealer for the recommended pressure. On cool days you can use the maximum figure. If the temperature is above 80° F (26° C), use a lower pressure, at least 5 pounds below maximum. If you weigh more than about 175 lb. (79 kg) or you are carrying a heavy load, increase recommended pressure by 5 to 10%. If the tire bulges more than slightly when loaded, it is under-inflated.

TIRE REPAIRS

Every cyclist will eventually experience trouble with a tire or tube. Repair and replacement are fairly simple and every rider should know the techniques. Tubular tire repair is more time consuming because it requires unstitching, restitching and gluing.

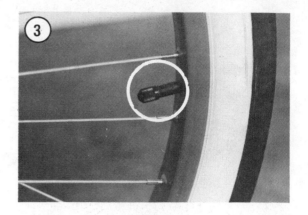

Patching a bicycle tube is only a temporary fix. The tire flexes so much that the patch will rub right off. However, a patched tube will get you far enough to buy a new tube.

Tire Repair Kits

Clincher tire repair kits can be purchased from bicycle dealers and some auto repair stores. When buying at stores other than

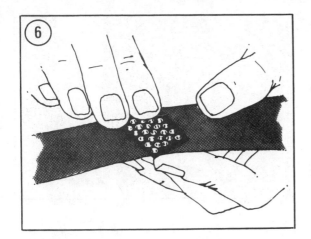

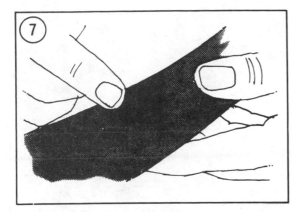

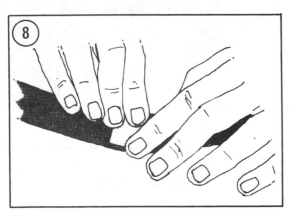

roadside repairs and the strength is unnecessary for a temporary repair.

Cold patches are not vulcanized to the tube; they are simply glued on. Though not as strong as hot patches, cold patches are still very durable. Cold patch kits are less bulky than hot and more easily applied under adverse conditions. Cold patch kits are best for emergency repairs on the road.

Tubular tire repair kits are found only at bicycle shops since tubulars require a much thinner patch material.

Cold Patch Repair

1. Remove tube from tire as described under *Clincher Tire Repair* in this chapter.
2. Roughen an area around the hole slightly larger than the patch (**Figure 6**). Use cap from repair kit or a pocket knife. Do not scrape too vigorously or you may cause additional damage.
3. Apply a small quantity of special cement to the puncture and spread it evenly with a finger (**Figure 7**).
4. Allow the cement to dry until tacky—usually 30 seconds or so is sufficient.
5. Remove the backing from the patch.

CAUTION
Do not touch the newly exposed rubber with your fingers or the patch will not stick firmly.

6. Center the patch over the hole. Hold the patch firmly in place for about 30 seconds to allow the cement to set (**Figure 8**).
7. Dust the patched area with talcum to prevent sticking.

Clincher Tire Repair

The following items are needed to repair a clincher tire and tube:
    a. Valve core remover.
    b. Cold patch repair kit.
    c. Sharp knife or razor blade.
    d. Chalk or crayon.
1. Remove the wheel from the bicycle.
2. Use a valve stem remover (**Figure 9**) and remove the valve core to deflate the tire.

bicycle dealers, specify that the kit you want is for bicycle tubes.

There are 2 types of tire repair kit for clincher tires:
    a. Hot patch.
    b. Cold patch.

Hot patches are strongest because they actually vulcanize to the tube, becoming part of it. However they are too bulky to carry for

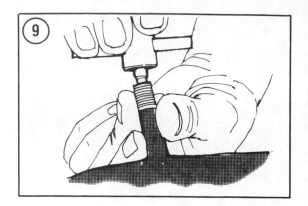

3. Insert a tire lever and lift a portion of the
bead over the wheel rim (**Figure 10**).
4. Continue lifting the bead over the rim with
additional tire levers until the entire bead is
off the rim.
5. Remove the tube from the tire.
6. Pull the tire free of the rim so that the
inside of the tire and rim can be thoroughly
inspected.
7. Reinstall the valve core and inflate tube
slightly. Do not over-inflate.
8. Immerse tube in water a section at a time
(**Figure 11**). Look carefully for bubbles
indicating a hole. Mark each hole and
continue checking until you are certain that
all holes are discovered and marked. Also
make sure that the valve core is not leaking;
tighten it if necessary.

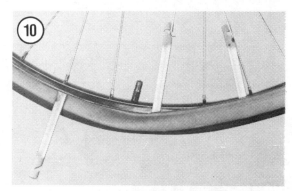

NOTE
*If you do not have enough water to
immerse sections of the tube, try
running your hand over the tube slowly
and very close to the surface. If your
hand is damp, it works even better. If
you suspect a hole anywhere, apply
some saliva to the area to verify it
(**Figure 12**).*

9. Apply a cold patch using the techniques
described under *Cold Patch Repair* in this
chapter.
10. Dust the patched area with talcum
powder to prevent it from sticking to the tire.
11. Carefully check inside the tire casing for
glass particles, thorns, nails or other objects
which may have damaged the tube. If inside
of tire is split, apply a patch to the area to
prevent it from pinching and damaging the
tube again.
12. Check the inside of the rim. Make sure
rim tape is in place and no spoke ends
protrude which could puncture the tube
(**Figure 13**).
13. Install one bead of the tire over the rim
(**Figure 14**).

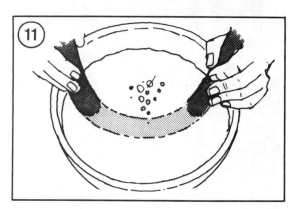

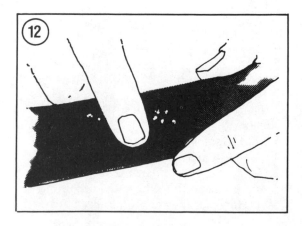

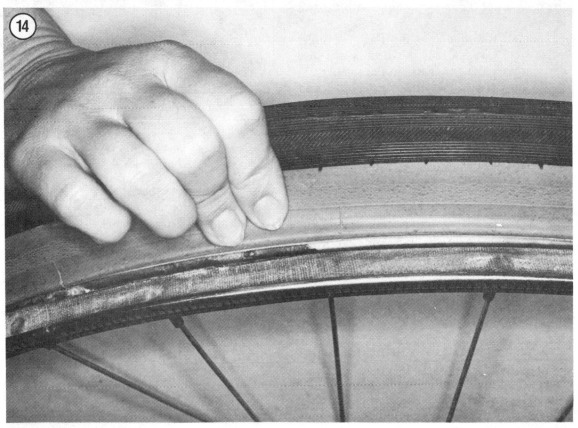

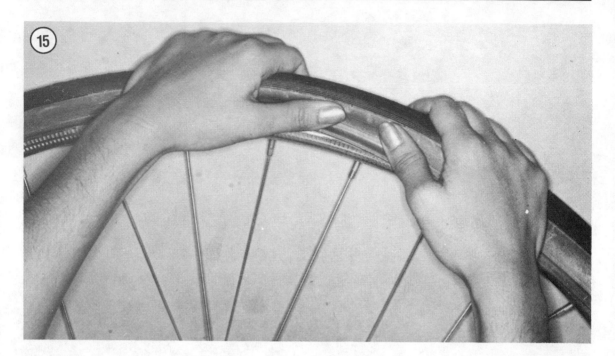

14. Inflate the tire just enough to round it out. Too much air will make it difficult to install it in the tire and too little will increase the chances of pinching the tube with the tire levers.

15. Install the tube into the tire and insert valve stem through hole in wheel. Make sure there are no folds or twists in the tube.

16. After tube is smoothed out and positioned completely around the rim, use your thumbs to push the tire bead back under rim (**Figure 15**).

17. Inflate the tire to the proper pressure. Refer to **Table 1** and check with a tire gauge (**Figure 16**).

Tubular Tire Repair

The following items are needed to repair tubular tires:

    a. Tubular tire repair kit.
    b. Talcum powder.
    c. Chalk.
    d. Emery cloth or extra fine sandpaper.
    e. X-acto knife, razor blade or sharp knife.
    f. Small section of 1/4 in. doweling, sanded smooth, or eraser-tipped pencil.

1. Remove the wheel from the bicycle.
2. Partially deflate the tire if it is not already flat.

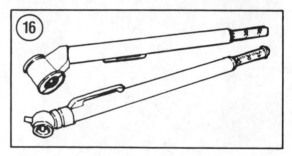

CAUTION
Do not use any type of metal tool for removing the tire from the rim or both the tire and the rim will be damaged.

3. To remove the tire:
    a. Apply force against sidewall with your thumbs (**Figure 17**). Apply force carefully and evenly.
    b. Work around the entire wheel and break the seal of the cement before removing any one portion of the tire.
    c. Remove the tire from the rim.

4. Submerge the tire in water and check for air bubbles indicating a leak. When a puncture or leak is found, dry and mark the spot with chalk.

5. Pull the rim tape away from the area to be repaired about 3-5 in. (75-125 mm) on either side of the puncture (**Figure 18**).

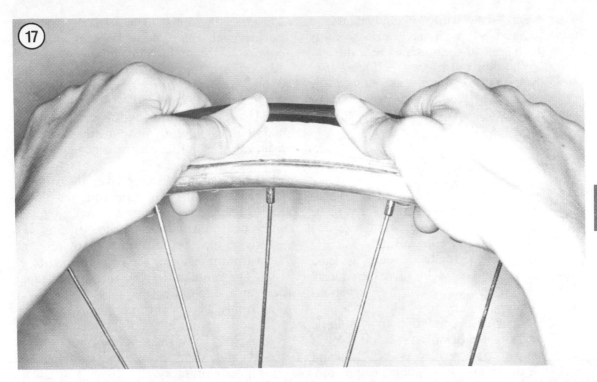

6. Use an X-acto knife or equivalant and position the blade with the sharp side away from the tube. Cut the stitching near the leak and pull the tube out of the tire (**Figure 19**).

7. Inspect the inside of the casing to see if the cause of puncture may still be inside or sticking through the casing. If an object is still present, remove it.

CAUTION
Take care to prevent any dirt or foreign particles from entering the casing.

8. Clean the exposed tube in the area to be patched. Rough the area with sandpaper. Do not allow this dust to enter casing.

9. Apply cement to the tube around the leak. Allow it to become tacky (a few minutes), then press on patch according to instructions in patch kit.

10. Check the casing wall and apply a fabric patch to the inside of wall if it is fractured. If the outside of tire has any cuts, etc., clean and seal with the special liquid rubber compound.

11. Dust the finished patch with talcum powder and place the tube back into the casing.

12. Smooth the protective tape inside the casing over the tube, then restitch using original holes (**Figure 20**).

13. Using a smooth blunt dowel or the eraser end of a pencil, gently poke the tube in, away from the stitching, so that it is not punctured by the needle (**Figure 21**).

14. Apply rubber cement over the stitches and reposition the protective rim tape.

15. Check the rim to be sure that no spoke ends protrude into the rim. If any do protrude, file the ends smooth to prevent them from puncturing the rim tape or tire.

16A. On tubular tires requiring rim tape, perform the following:

    a. Apply 2 coats of rim cement to the rim. Let it set for about 20-30 minutes.

    b. Apply the rim tape to the rim.

    c. Apply a coat of rim cement to tape. Let it set until tacky.

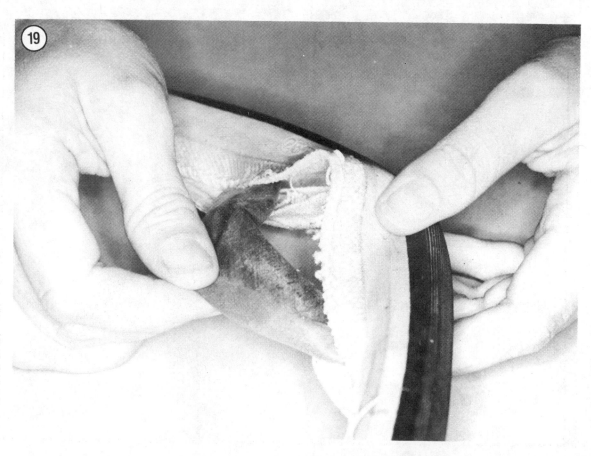

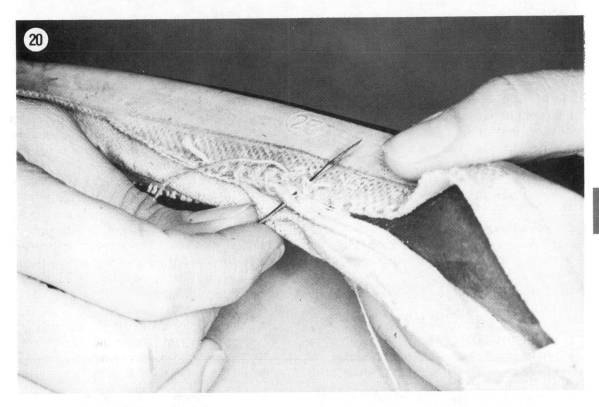

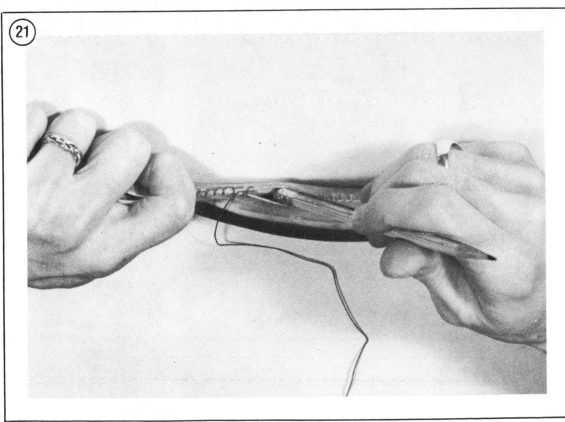

16B. On tubular tires cemented directly to rim without rim tape, perform the following:
   a. Clean rim and file spoke ends.
   b. Apply cement to rim.
17. Deflate the tire.
18. With wheel in the upright position, insert air valve through hole in rim.
19. Position the tire onto the rim by working down either side from the top.
20. Inflate the tire to about 1/2 of the recommended air pressure, just enough to give it shape to position and seat the tire correctly on the rim.
21. Install the wheel.
22. Inflate the tire to the proper pressure. Refer to **Table 2** and check with a tire gauge (**Figure 16**).

WHEELS

Wire wheels are used on most bicycles. These consist of a rim, spokes and a hub. The rim either has a deep U-shaped channel for clincher tires or a slight depression for tubular tires. The spokes support the rim on the hub and are adjustable so that the wheel can be made to run true without wobbling. The hubs are described in detail in Chapter Six and Chapter Seven.

Mag type wheels (**Figure 22**) are sometimes used on BMX bicycles. This wheel is stronger than a wire wheel but weighs a little more. The use of this type of wheel is strictly personal preference.

Front Wheel
Removal/Installation

1. Mount the bicycle in a repair stand or have someone hold the front wheel off the ground.
2. On wheels with caliper brakes, make sure that the brake pads are separated far enough to remove the wheel. Perform the following:
   a. On bicycles so equipped, move the quick release hand lever (**Figure 23**) or quick release device on the brake cable.

NOTE
During the next step, do not let the cable end slip out of the cable anchor bolt; it's difficult to thread the cable back in.

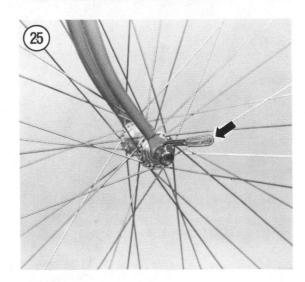

b. On models without a quick-release device, loosen the cable anchor bolt (**Figure 24**) on the brake caliper, slacken the cable and open the brakes.

3A. On front wheels with quick-release hubs, unlock the lever (**Figure 25**) so that it points straight out.

3B. On front wheels with ordinary nuts or wing nuts, use 2 wrenches and loosen both nuts simultaneously.

4. Pull the wheel down and out of the fork slots.

5. Installation is the reverse of these steps. Adjust the brake calipers if the cable was loosened in Step 2.

4

**Rear Wheel
Removal**

1. Mount the bicycle in a repair stand or have someone hold the rear wheel off the ground.

2. On wheels with caliper brakes, make sure that the brake pads are separated far enough to remove the wheel. Perform the following:

a. On bicycles so equipped, move the quick-release hand lever (A, **Figure 26**) or quick-release device on the brake cable.

NOTE
During the next step, do not let the cable end slip out of the cable anchor bolt; it's difficult to thread the cable back in.

b. On models without a quick-release device, loosen the cable anchor bolt (B, **Figure 26**) on the brake caliper and slacken the cable and open the brakes.

3A. On bicycles with a coaster brake, remove screw and nut (A, **Figure 27**) clamping the end of the brake arm to the frame.

3B. On multi-speed hubs, shift to high gear and loosen the locknut (A, **Figure 28**) on the cable adjusting sleeve. Unscrew the sleeve (B, **Figure 28**) until the cable is free.

CAUTION
During the next step, shift gears only while rear wheel and pedals are in motion or the derailleur may be damaged.

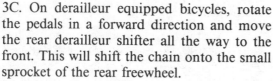

3C. On derailleur equipped bicycles, rotate the pedals in a forward direction and move the rear derailleur shifter all the way to the front. This will shift the chain onto the small sprocket of the rear freewheel.

4A. On rear wheels with quick-release hubs, unlock the lever (**Figure 29**) so that it points straight out.

4B. On rear wheels held by ordinary nuts (B, **Figure 27**) or wing nuts, use 2 wrenches and loosen both nuts simultaneously.

5A. On derailleur equipped bicycles, check that the chain is on the smallest sprocket. Push the rear wheel down and forward while holding the derailleur back away from the wheel. Do not remove derailleur.

5B. On all other models, pull the wheel down and out of the slots in the frame. Slip the chain off the rear sprocket.

Rear Wheel
Installation

1. On models without quick-release levers, if removed, install the nuts on the axle ends very loosely.

2. On derailleur equipped models, make sure the gear shifter is still positioned as during *Removal* Step 3C.

3A. On derailleur equipped bicycles *without* quick-release hubs, perform the following:
  a. Install the wheel axle into the slots in frame.

b. Slip the chain over the *smallest* sprocket.
c. Push axle all the way into the slots and tighten the nuts only finger-tight.
d. Keep the right-hand end of the axle (nearest the derailleur) firmly seated.
e. Move the other end of the axle in its slot until the wheel is centered between the chain stays.
f. Tighten the nuts securely with the wheel in this position.

3B. On derailleur equipped bicycles *with* quick-release hubs, perform the following:
  a. Loosen the lever 2 or 3 turns.
  b. Slip the chain over the *smallest* sprocket.
  c. Push the axle all the way into the slots.
  d. Keep the right-hand end of the axle (nearest the derailleur) firmly seated.
  e. Move the other end of the axle in its slot until the wheel is centered between the chain stays.
  f. Lock the quick-release lever while holding the wheel in position. If the lever locks relatively easily, unlock it and tighten the adjusting nut on the opposite end of the axle a few turns.
  g. Center the wheel again and lock the lever. Repeat step if necessary until the lever is relatively hard to lock.

3C. On all other models, perform the following:

4

a. Fit chain over rear wheel sprocket.
b. Install the axle ends in the slots in the frame.
c. Pull the wheel back until the chain has about 1/2 in. (13 mm) of play (**Figure 30**).
d. Make sure that the wheel rim is centered between the chain stays. Hold the wheel in this position and tighten the axle nuts.
4. On multi-speed hubs, reconnect the gear change cable and adjust as described in Chapter Three.
5. On coaster brakes, secure the brake arm to the frame and tighten the bolt and nuts securely.
6. Adjust the caliper brakes if the cable anchor bolt was loosened in *Removal* Step 2.

Spoke Replacement

If 1 or 2 spokes are broken and the wheel wobbles only slightly, the broken spokes can be replaced. If you do not feel qualified to replace more than a couple of spokes, take the wheel to a dealer. If the wheel is really tweaked out of shape, it is cheaper to purchase a new wheel than to have a dealer relace all of the spokes.

You will need a spoke wrench (**Figure 31**) of the correct size for this procedure. Some spoke wrenches have several different sizes in one tool.

1. Remove the wheel from the bicycle and remove the tire from the rim as described in this chapter.
2. Using a spoke wrench, remove the broken spoke pieces.
3. On derailleur equipped models, remove the freewheel cluster if the broken spoke is on the same side as the cluster. Refer to Chapter Six.
4. Using a spoke wrench, remove a good spoke *from the same side of wheel* as the broken spoke(s).
5. Take the good spoke to a bicycle dealer and purchase replacement spoke of exactly the same length, thickness and nipple type.
6. Stick the new spoke through the hole in the hub. Note that the heads of the spokes alternate between inside and outside of hub (**Figure 32**).

7. Insert the spoke end into the hole in the rim. If replacing more than one spoke, make sure that it conforms to the pattern of all other spokes on the wheel.

8. Install the nipple on the end of the spoke and tighten finger-tight.

9. Install the wheel in the frame temporarily.

10. Adjust spoke tension as described in this chapter, without the tire installed.

11. After the spoke tension is correct, remove the wheel from the frame and remount the tire as described in this chapter.

Spoke Adjustment

Wheels that wobble may be trued by adjusting spoke tension. Ideally, all spokes should have the same tension. This is very difficult to achieve without experience and special equipment. Take all such jobs to a bicycle dealer or follow the wheel alignment procedure in this chapter. Indiscriminate spoke adjustment will cause more wobble than it will cure.

If you have replaced 1 or 2 spokes, you may be able to adjust spoke tension yourself. First get some idea about the tension of the other spokes.

1. One method is as follows:
   a. Pluck each spoke with your finger like a guitar string. Note the sound made by the spokes.
   b. Tighten the new spoke until the sound matches the others.

2. Another method is to examine the end of the old spokes where they enter the nipples.
   a. If there are threads visible, count them.
   b. Tighten new spokes until the same number of threads are visible.

3. Still another method is to tighten, then loosen, several old spokes about 1/8 turn.
   a. Try to feel the force required to turn the nipple.
   b. Tighten the new spoke until the same force is required to turn the nipple.
   c. Keep track of exactly how much you move the old nipples; they must be returned to the same position when you are done.

4. After adjusting the spokes, check that the ends do not protrude past the nipple; they

might puncture the tube. If necessary, file the end of the spoke down.

5. Install the wheel temporarily without the tire.

6. Spin it and check for wobble. If wobble is excessive, try to true it as described in this chapter.

Wheel Lacing

> *NOTE*
> *If the wheel is really tweaked out of shape or damaged, it is cheaper to purchase a new wheel rather than have a dealer relace all the spokes, unless you have a very expensive hub on the wheel.*

Relacing a wheel is not difficult if you work patiently and carefully. If you doubt your ability to do either, leave the job to an experienced bicycle mechanic; you will save yourself countless hours of frustration.

A knowledge of lacing can save you a considerable amount of money. You can replace a damaged hub or rim for the cost of the part alone or you can purchase an exotic rim and hub combination and lace your own custom wheels.

Spokes are these thin wires that support you and the bicycle. A spoke is actually a threaded stud connected to the hub by its head and to the rim by the nipple that passes through the rim from the outside. The nipple is usually made of brass; the spoke is made of zinc plated steel or stainless steel. Spokes are either a straight-gauge type with a uniform thickness from end to end or they are butted (**Figure 33**). A butted spoke is thinner in the middle and thicker at each end where the stress is greater. Spokes differ in diameter and length according to your specific needs and wheel configuration.

When purchasing new spokes from a bicycle dealer always take in your rim, hub and spokes in order to be assured of purchasing the correct spokes. You can purchase spokes by themselves or with nipples included (**Figure 34**). When buying nipples, get ones with a slot in the end for a screwdriver. The best spoke for all-around use is made of zinc-plated medium-carbon

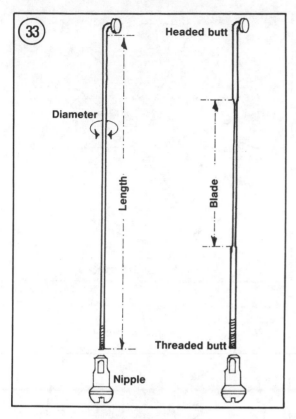

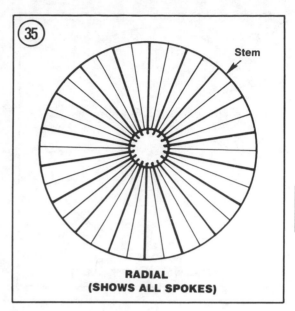

RADIAL
(SHOWS ALL SPOKES)

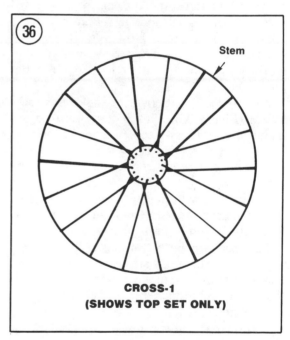

CROSS-1
(SHOWS TOP SET ONLY)

steel. They are the least expensive but will last the longest. Chrome plated spokes look nice but are brittle and will break easily. Stainless steel spokes are also pleasing to the eye but are also weak and brittle and tend to break fairly easy.

Lacing Patterns

There are many patterns in use. Each pattern is identified by the number of other spokes a single spoke crosses between the hub and the rim.

With the radial pattern, spokes do not cross each other at all (**Figure 35**). This type of wheel is easy to lace and true, but it lacks the strength of other types. Use this pattern for lightness only on non-driving wheels, such as the front wheel on brakeless racing bicycles.

Figure 36 shows a cross-1 pattern. Note that each spoke crosses one other spoke

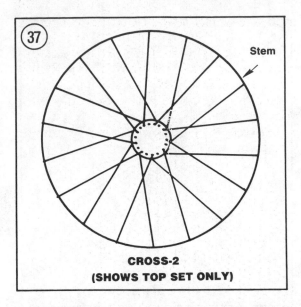

CROSS-2
(SHOWS TOP SET ONLY)

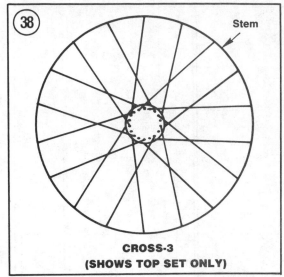

CROSS-3
(SHOWS TOP SET ONLY)

between hub and rim. This pattern is slightly heavy than radial spoking because longer spokes are required. However, it is also stronger. Use a cross-1 spoke pattern only on non-driving wheels with no brake or with caliper brake.

With a cross-2 pattern, each spoke crosses 2 others (**Figure 37**). This pattern is stronger than radial or cross-1 spoking, but still is not strong enough for a driving wheel. Use it for front wheels with no front brake or a caliper brake.

The cross-3 pattern is most popular (**Figure 38**). It is used for both front and rear wheels with either kind of brake (coaster or caliper).

The cross-4 pattern is strongest (**Figure 39**). It requires the longest spokes and is the heaviest. Cross-4 spoking is most common on the rear wheel of tandem bicycles, because of its strength.

If you are relacing or replacing an old wheel note which lacing pattern is used. It is usually best to use the same pattern when relacing.

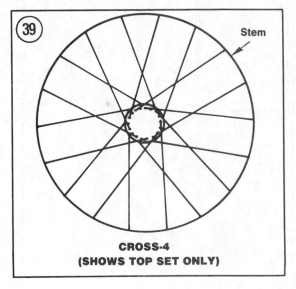

CROSS-4
(SHOWS TOP SET ONLY)

Wheel Lacing Procedure

1. Remove the tire and the rim strip.
2A. On rear wheels equipped with a derailleur, remove the freewheel cluster from the wheel as described in Chapter Six.
2B. On rear wheels equipped with a multi-speed hub, remove the multi-speed hub

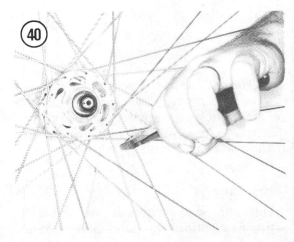

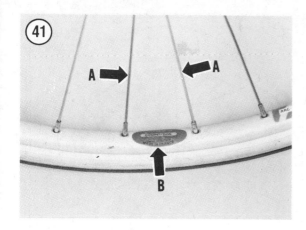

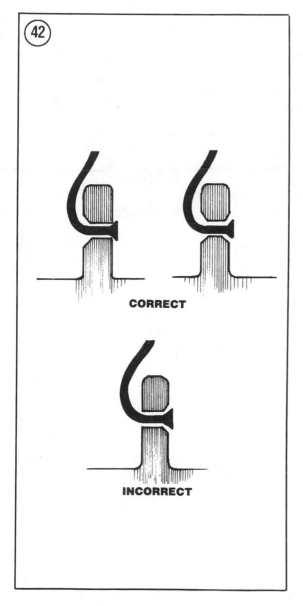

CORRECT

INCORRECT

from the wheel as described in Chapter Seven.

3. Note the pattern of the spokes (radial, cross-1, etc.), then cut all spokes from the hub with a strong wire cutter (**Figure 40**).

4. Remove the spoke halves from the hub and the rim.

5. Unscrew the nipples from the spokes and save them if undamaged.

CAUTION
Spoke ends which protrude from the nipple are usually ground off to prevent tire damage. This often leaves a burr which can destroy the nipple threads when it is unscrewed.

6. Plan the lacing pattern so that the 2 spokes (A, **Figure 41**) next to the manufacturer's sticker (B, **Figure 41**) are pulling toward the sticker, not away from it. This sticker is usually placed over the rim seam where the rim is welded together. If the spokes are pulling away from the seam, it will tend to separate.

7. Get in a comfortable position (cross-legged on the floor) with all of the wheel parts near you.

8. Insert one spoke through any hole in the hub. The spoke must exit on the side of the hub with the countersink. If the spoke exits the sharp side the hole will tend to cut into the spoke causing it to fracture and eventually break. **Figure 42** shows the correct and incorrect way to insert spokes in the hub.

NOTE
Most modern hubs have countersunk holes. If your hub is not countersunk, purchase a blunt-tapered hand reamer from an auto supply store or hardware store. Bevel the holes in the hub by hand.

9. Insert the installed spoke end through the rim hole and screw the nipple on about 3 turns. Note correct location of valve stem hole. If located improperly, fitting a tire pump will be difficult (**Figure 43**).

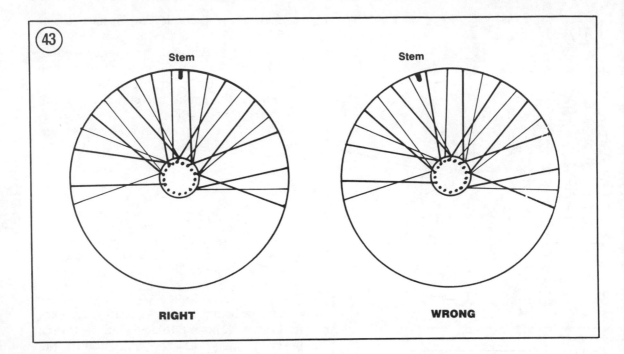

10. Starting with the first spoke, install additional spokes in every other hub hole and every 4th rim hole (**Figure 44**). Insert the spokes into the hub from the same direction as the first one. Screw on the nipples 3 or 4 turns each.

11. On all patterns except radial, hold the rim and turn the hub so the installed spokes radiate clockwise from the hub to the rim (**Figure 45**).

12. Insert the second set of spokes into the remaining hub holes in the direction opposite the first set. That is, the spoke heads for the second set will be on the opposite side of the hub flange from the first set.

13. Select any spoke from the second set and perform the following:

    a. For a radial pattern, insert the threaded end through the rim, 2 holes clockwise from the spoke in the adjacent hub hole (**Figure 46**).

    b. For a cross-spoking, lay the spoke *behind* the first set so that it radiates counterclockwise from the hub. After crossing the appropriate number of spokes in the first set, insert the spoke through the rim hole halfway between 2 spokes of the first set. Refer to **Figures 36-39**. Thread on the nipple 3 or 4 turns.

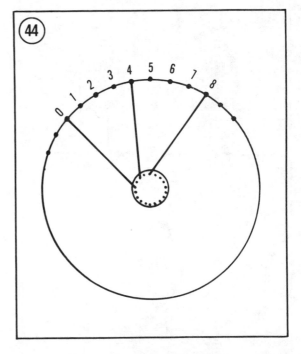

14. Repeat Step 13 until all spokes of the second set are installed. When you complete this step, each spoke will cross the same number of other spokes, every hub hole on one flange will be occupied and every other rim hole will be occupied. Spoke heads will alternate between inside and outside of flange.

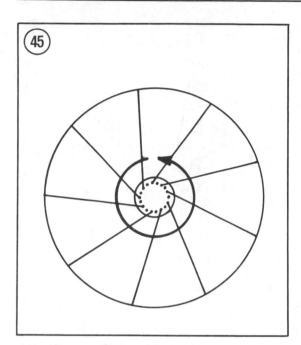

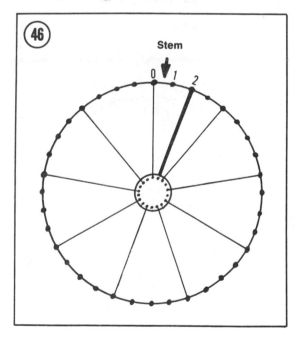

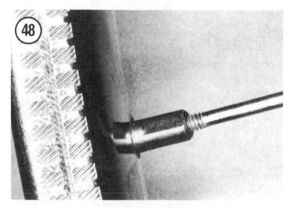

15. Turn the wheel over and install the other 2 sets of spokes in the same manner as the first 2 sets.

16. Install wheel in bicycle fork or truing stand.

17. Squirt a very small amount of Trifilon or other type of oil onto the nipple head and end of the spoke. This will allow the spokes to be tightened evenly.

18. Tighten each spoke gradually and evenly a few turns at a time until all nipples just touch the rim and the wheel is centered.

19. True the wheel as described in this chapter.

Wheel Truing

Wheel truing or alignment can be an exasperating experience unless you have patience and take your time. The job cannot be done quickly.

To do the job properly, you must have a truing stand (**Figure 47**). Several commercial stands are available but they are relatively expensive. It may be cheaper to have the wheel trued by a bicycle dealer than to buy a truing stand. You can build your own truing stand as described in Chapter Two.

1. Make sure the axle cones are properly adjusted as described in Chapter Six.

2. Mount the wheel in the truing stand.

3. If the wheel has just been relaced, tighten all nipples evenly until about 4 or 5 threads show under the nipples (**Figure 48**). Tighten all inside spokes first, then all outside spokes.

4. If working on a rear wheel equipped with a freewheel cluster, tighten spokes on the freewheel side 2 or 3 additional turns. This helps to "dish" or flatten the freewheel side.

5. Pluck each spoke as you would a guitar string. All spokes should emit the same pitch. Readjust the spoke tension as necessary to get the pitch close on all spokes.

6. Rotate the wheel and watch it closely. Look for side-to-side wobble or out-of-round hopping. Also make sure that the rim is centered between the ends of the cone locknuts (**Figure 49**) so that the wheel assembly will be on the centerline of the chainstay and the bicycle.

NOTE

*Do not center the rim on the hub (**Figure 50**). This is very important on "dished" rear wheels equipped with freewheels. If you center the rim on the hub, the wheel assembly will be offset toward the left and away from the centerline of the chainstay and the bicycle.*

7. If the wheel does not run true, use the following procedures to correct the condition.

To correct side-to-side wobble

1. Spin the wheel slowly in a truing stand.
2. Hold a piece of chalk or crayon so that it just touches the side of the rim. Mark high spots.
3. Slightly loosen the spokes closest to mark on the marked side of rim. Tighten the spokes near the mark on unmarked side of rim (**Figure 51**).

NOTE

Loosen or tighten no more than one turn at a time.

4. Repeat this procedure for each marked area as often as necessary to eliminate all side wobble.

To correct out-of-round

1. Hold a piece of chalk or crayon so that it just clears the inner surface of the rim.
2. Spin the wheel slowly in truing stand.
3. Mark any high spots with chalk or crayon.

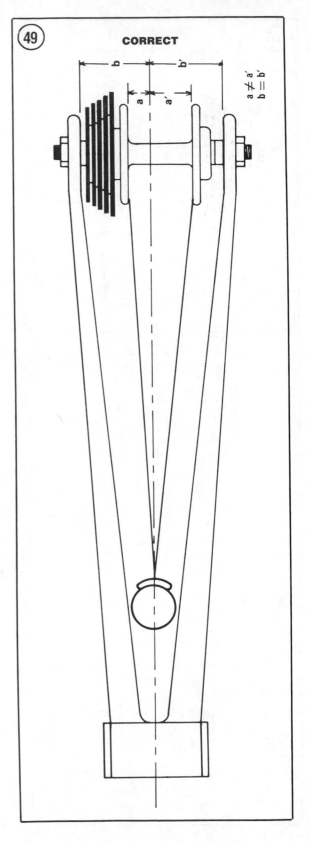

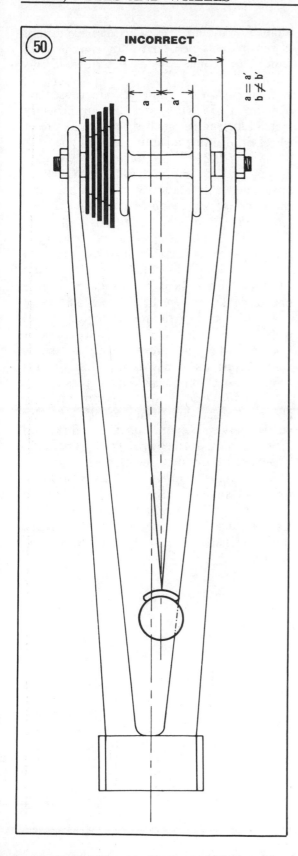

INCORRECT

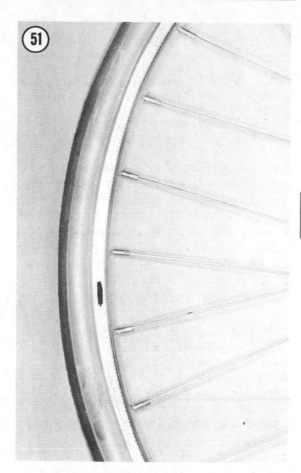

4. Hold the chalk or crayon so that it just clears the inner surface of the rim.

5. Mark any low spots with chalk or crayon.

6. Loosen all spokes around the low spot; loosen the ones near the middle of the spot more than the others.

7. Tighten all spokes around the high spot; tighten those near the middle of the spot more than the others.

8. Repeat procedure as often as necessary to eliminate the out-of-round condition.

To center wheel between locknuts

1. Mount the wheel in a truing stand.

2. Measure the distance between the center of the rim and the locknut on both sides (B, **Figure 49**).

3. If they are unequal, loosen all spokes on the short side and tighten all spokes on the long side until the rim is centered.

NOTE
Loosen or tighten all spokes evenly and
no more than one turn at a time.

4. Repeat this procedure as often as necessary. Check for out-of-round and side wobble as described in this chapter.

TROUBLES

Probably the most common roadway dangers for tires, tubes and wheels are chuckholes, curbs, rocks, etc. These road hazards can rupture or puncture the tube or dent the rim. Although a rupture may not cause a flat right away, the tube may be pinched, causing a slow leak. A nicked or dented wheel may create abrasion which will eventually wear through a tire and tube.

1. *Rim cuts*—Rim cuts are usually caused by underinflation and/or heavy loads. The wheel rim chafes against the tire wall and wears a hole in the tire.

2. *Abrasion*—If wheels are not aligned, tires can chafe on front forks and rear wheel stays. Abrasion can also be caused by striking the wall of the tire against a curb or similar object.

3. *Star breaks*—These are only visible from inside the tire and are caused by punctures from nails, sharp stones, glass or other objects.

4. *Broken beads*—Beads are broken most often by clumsy or improper efforts to remove or mount tires. This damage cannot be repaired. Use your hands or a tire lever to remove or mount tires as described in this Chapter.

5. *Blowouts*—Most blowouts are caused by over-inflation. However, an improperly seated tube can be pinched against the tire or wheel rim causing a rupture in the tube.

6. *Uneven tire wear*—Uneven tire wear is usually caused by a crooked wheel or misaligned wheel hub. Spin the wheel and check for excessive wobble at the rim. Have a bicycle dealer true the wheel or replace it. Worn flat spots are normally caused by skidding stops which should be avoided.

7. *Wheel wobble*—Wheel wobble occurs when the rim is bent or misaligned due to uneven spoke tension. Take wheel to a bicycle dealer for truing or replacement. Wheel wobble may also occur when hub cones or axle mounting nuts are loose or the axle is bent. Adjust the cones as described in this chapter. Check mounting nut tightness.

8. *Tire rubs frame*—Wheel is not properly aligned. Loosen the left mounting nut, center wheel between chain stays or fork and retighten nut. If the wheel still rubs, spin wheel and check for wobble.

9. *Hub binds, grabs, or makes unusual noises*—Usually caused by dirt or grit in bearings or by cones which are too tight. May also be caused by broken or bent hub parts. Refer to Chapter Six and Chapter Seven.

Table 1 CLINCHER TIRE PRESSURE

Size (in.)	Pressure (psi)
16×1 3/8	35-45
16×1.75	30-40
20×1 3/8	35-45
20×1.75	30-40
20×2.125	30-35
24×1 3/8	40-45
24×1.75	30-40
24×2.125	35-45
26×1 3/8	45-50
26×1.75	30-40
26×2.125	35-45
27×1 1/4	75-85

Size (mm)	Fits rim size	Pressure (psi)
700×75C	27×1	110
700×28	27×1 1/8	100
700×32C	27×1 1/4	80

4

Table 2 TUBULAR TIRE PRESSURE

Type of riding	Pressure Front	Rear
Track racing (smooth)	85-115	90-120
Track racing (uneven)	75-95	80-100
Road racing	65-90	80-100
Touring	75-90	85-100

CHAPTER FIVE

BRAKES

Cycling can only be as safe as your brakes. Brakes that slip, stick or don't work at all invite damage to the bicycle and injury to you. Understanding how your brakes work and how to keep them in good repair is very important. Brakes may be hand- or foot-operated. Most single-speed bicycles have a single foot-operated coaster brake. Many bicycles with multi-speed rear hubs have a coaster brake for the rear wheel and a hand-operated caliper brake on the front. Other multi-speed hub bicycles and all derailleur type bicycles have hand-operated caliper brakes front and rear.

Coaster brakes are foot-operated by back pedaling. The brake parts are an integral part of the rear hub. Rear hubs are relatively complex, but fortunately coaster brakes give very little trouble when properly maintained as described in Chapter Three. They require no routine adjustments and have no delicate connecting cables, making them ideal for children's bicycles.

Caliper hand brakes work similar to automobile disc brakes. When you squeeze the hand lever, rubber pads are forced against the side of the wheel rim.

There are 3 major types of caliper hand brakes:

a. Side-pull caliper.
b. Center-pull caliper.
c. Cantilever caliper.

All 3 types force the brake shoes against the wheel rim. The difference lies in the method and precision with which they operate.

Center-pull calipers usually operate more smoothly and evenly than side-pull calipers on wheels that are not perfectly true (**Figure 1**). As the brake lever is squeezed, the main cable pulls up on a short transverse cable. This in turn pulls evenly on both brake arms. The brake shoes, therefore, press evenly against the wheel rim.

Side-pull calipers are similar to center-pull calipers, but are pulled on one side only (**Figure 2**). Side-pull calipers can be manufactured for less money than comparable quality center-pull calipers. However, some of the best calipers made are side-pull calipers.

Cantilever brakes are similar to center-pull calipers but they are mounted differently on the frame. There are individual levers that mount on pivot shafts on the fork or seat stays. The main advantage of cantilever brakes is that they have better leverage and are able to exert more force onto the bicycle rim. As the brake lever is squeezed, the main cable pulls up on a short transverse cable. This in turn pulls evenly on both brake arms. The brake shoes, therefore, press evenly against the wheel rim.

This chapter describes repair procedures for all brake systems. There is an exploded view drawing that shows a typical assembly of each of the 3 brake types. Due to the number of major manufacturers and all of the different models that each one produces it would be difficult to represent all of them in this chapter. All modern brake systems are similar in design with only slight variations.

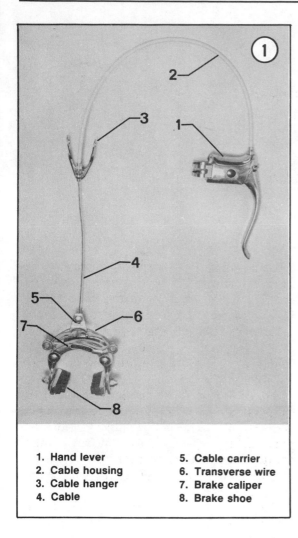

1. Hand lever
2. Cable housing
3. Cable hanger
4. Cable
5. Cable carrier
6. Transverse wire
7. Brake caliper
8. Brake shoe

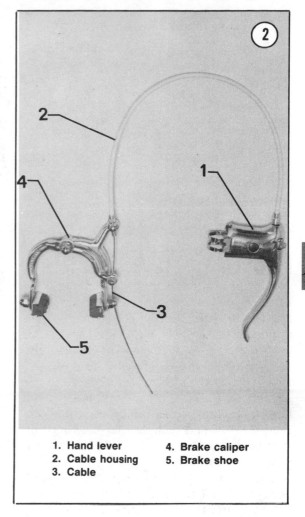

1. Hand lever
2. Cable housing
3. Cable
4. Brake caliper
5. Brake shoe

5

Unless you have a very expensive caliper brake assembly on your bicycle, it is usually cheaper to replace the entire assembly than to try to find replacement parts for it. Many bicycle dealers do not even carry replacement parts for most brakes.

COASTER BRAKES

Coaster brakes are part of the rear hub assembly. In most cases, the rear hub is complicated and requires special tools and/or special knowledge to repair. Refer to Chapter Seven for advice on these brakes. Refer to Chapter Three for routine maintenance.

HAND LEVERS

There are many makes of hand levers used, but all are similar. The main differences occur in the method of attaching the brake cable to the lever. For BMX racing there are some trick levers (**Figure 3**) with special bends and recesses for the fingers. Hand levers on low-priced bicycles are held onto the handlebar clamp with a single external screw

(**Figure 4**). Hand levers on turned-down handlebars attach to a clamp by a pull-up nut or screw inside the lever post (**Figure 5**).

Cables attach to hand levers in either of 2 ways. On some types, the end of the lever is slotted so that the cable can readily be disconnected and connected. On other levers, the entire cable must be threaded through a hole in the lever; the lever end of the cable has a lead piece to secure the end.

Some hand levers have a quick-release feature. Depressing a button on the lever permits the lever to be opened wider than normal (**Figure 6**). This opens the caliper wider than normal so that the wheel can be removed without disturbing the brakes.

The following procedure represents typical hand levers found on most modern bicycles.

Removal/Installation

1. Squeeze the brake shoes against the wheel rim with a "third hand" (**Figure 7**) or have a helper squeeze them.

2A. On side-pull brakes, loosen the cable anchor bolt and pull the cable out enough so the hand lever moves freely (**Figure 8**). Don't pull the cable completely out of the anchor

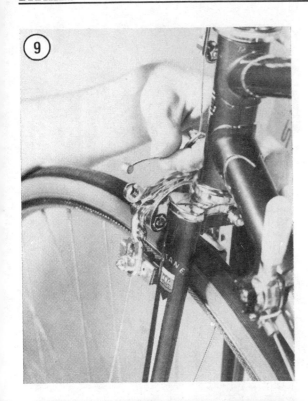

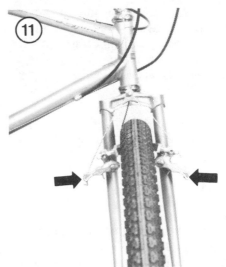

bolt if possible; sometimes it is difficult to thread back in.

2B. On some center-pull brakes, one end of the short transverse cable can be disconnected. Disconnect as shown (**Figure 9**).

2C. On center-pull brakes with no quick-release lever and no easy method of disconnecting transverse cable, loosen the cable anchor bolt (**Figure 10**).

2D. On cantilever brakes, disconnect the cable from each brake lever (**Figure 11**).

2E. On brakes with a quick-release lever on the cable hanger (such as Campagnolo Record), pull up on the lever to slacken the cable.

3A. On an upright handlebar, loosen the screw clamping the hand lever and slide the lever off (**Figure 4**).

3B. On turned-down handlebars, squeeze the hand lever. Loosen the screw (**Figure 5**) or nut inside, but do not remove it. Remove the hand lever.

4. Disconnect the cable from the lever. On slotted levers, line up the cable with the slot and lift out the leaded end. On other levers, pull the entire cable out of the cable housing and hand lever after disconnecting it from the brake caliper.

5. Install by reversing these removal steps, noting the following.

6. On hand levers with a hole, thread the entire cable through the hole. Grease the

cable lightly with Lubriplate and thread it through the cable housing. Continually twist the cable *counterclockwise* while threading it to keep the cable end from unraveling.

7. Adjust the brakes as described in Chapter Three.

CABLES

The cables connect to the hand lever at one end and to the brake caliper at the other as shown in **Figure 1** and **Figure 2**. The cables run through a housing with ferrules at each end and they are adjustable.

Replacement

1. Loosen the cable anchor bolt on the brake caliper. See **Figure 10** and **Figure 12**.
2. Pull the cable out from the hand lever end. On slotted levers, disconnect the cable from the lever before removing the cable.
3. Take the old cable to a bicycle dealer. Select a new cable at least as long as the old one or longer. Never buy one that is shorter. Make sure the hand lever end has the proper shaped leaded end.
4. Carefully examine the cable housing. Check for kinks or bends, particularly at the ferrules. If the ends are damaged, cut them off cleanly:
   a. Cut through the outer covering with a knife.
   b. With wire cutters, cut the end of the housing off between the coils.
   c. If you leave a burr, it will eventually cut into your cable; snip or file it off.
5. If the cable housing is damaged, replace it:
   a. On some bicycles, the housing is held to the frame with clips (**Figure 13**). Loosen or remove the clips and remove the housing.
   b. Purchase a length of cable housing slightly longer than the original; you can always cut it shorter to fit.
   c. Make sure that your ferrules fit the new housing; if not, purchase new ferrules to fit.
   d. Cut the new cable housing exactly as long as the original housing.
   e. Install the housing through the frame clips, if they are present.
   f. Place the ferrules on the ends of the cable housing.

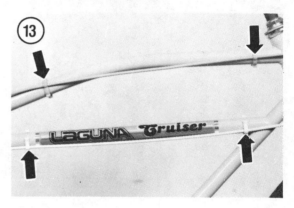

6A. On slotted levers, grease the cable lightly with Lubriplate and thread it through the cable housing. Continually twist the cable *counterclockwise* while threading to prevent the cable from unraveling. Connect the cable to the hand lever.

6B. On levers with a hole, thread the entire cable through the hole. Grease the cable lightly with Lubriplate and thread it through the cable housing. Continually twist the cable while threading it to keep cable end from unraveling.

7. Hold tension on the brake mechanism end of the cable with your hand. Work the hand lever back and forth and make sure that the cable and lever work smoothly.

8. Thread the cable into the cable anchor bolt on the brake mechanism. Do not cut off excess cable until after you have adjusted brakes.

9. Adjust brakes as described in Chapter Three.

SIDE-PULL CALIPERS

There are many side-pull brakes manufactured for bicycles. **Figure 14** shows

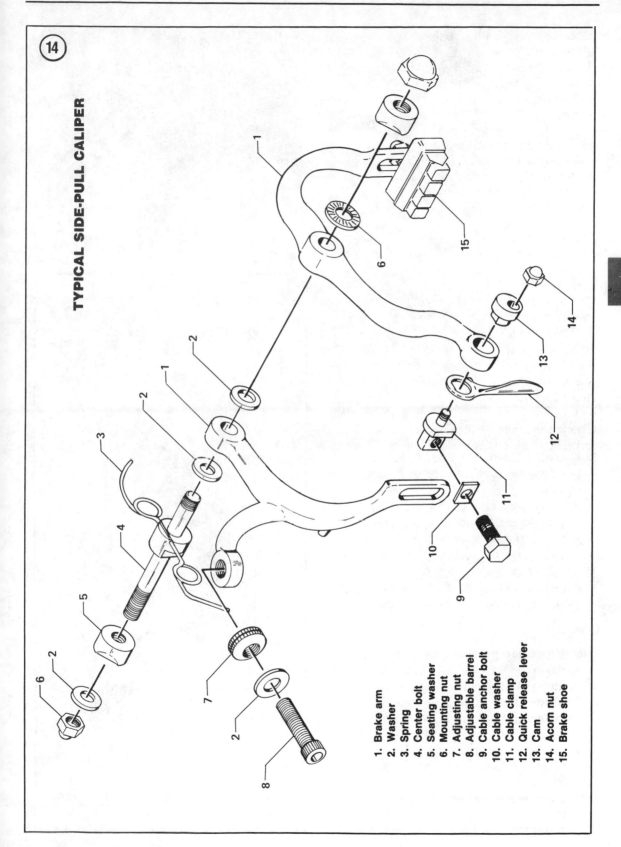

TYPICAL SIDE-PULL CALIPER

1. Brake arm
2. Washer
3. Spring
4. Center bolt
5. Seating washer
6. Mounting nut
7. Adjusting nut
8. Adjustable barrel
9. Cable anchor bolt
10. Cable washer
11. Cable clamp
12. Quick release lever
13. Cam
14. Acorn nut
15. Brake shoe

5

an exploded view of a typical side-pull caliper. If your caliper varies from this illustration, make a simple sketch of it as you disassemble it; most likely you will find it is built exactly like the one shown with the exception of a couple of small items.

Removal/Installation

1. Loosen the cable anchor bolt and disconnect the cable (**Figure 8**).
2. Remove the mounting nut (**Figure 15**) or Allen bolt (**Figure 16**), washer and concave washer (optional) holding the brake caliper to the frame.
3. Remove the brake caliper assembly.
4. Installation is the reverse of these steps. Center the brakes so that both brake shoes are the same distance from the rim before tightening mounting nut (**Figure 17**).
5. Adjust brake shoe position and cable length as described in Chapter Three.

Overhaul

Replacement parts for calipers are very difficult to find. Before performing an overhaul, determine if parts are available. Unless you have a very expensive caliper brake assembly on your bicycle, it is usually cheaper to replace the entire assembly than to try to find replacement parts for it. Many bicycle dealers do not even carry replacement parts for most brakes.

If the caliper merely needs a good cleaning or if you have a source of replacement parts, use the following procedure.

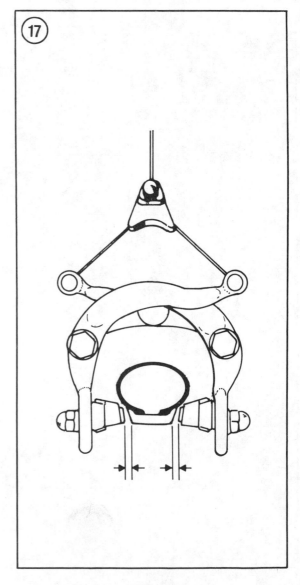

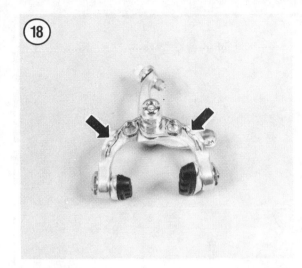

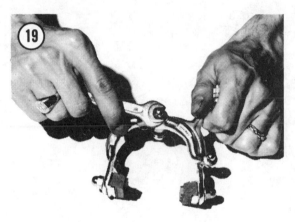

8. Assemble all parts on the pivot bolt by reversing the order in Step 5. Follow your sketch or see the exploded view diagram in **Figure 14**.

9. Install the locknut and perform the following:
   a. Tighten the locknut against the arms.
   b. Back the nut off (counterclockwise) 1/2 turn.
   c. Hold the locknut in position with a wrench and tighten the acorn nut against it.

10. Hold the ends of the springs with gas pliers and pry them over the stops and onto the brake arms.

11. Install the brake caliper assembly as described in this chapter.

12. Connect the cable to the cable anchor bolt and adjust as described in Chapter Three.

CENTER-PULL CALIPERS

There are many of center-pull brakes manufactured for bicycles. **Figure 20** shows an exploded view of a typical center-pull caliper. If your caliper varies from this illustration, make a simple sketch of it as you disassemble it; most likely you will find it is built exactly like the one shown with the exception of a couple of small items.

1. Remove the caliper from the bicycle as described in this chapter.

2. Pry the spring ends off the stops on the brake arms (**Figure 18**).

3. Remove the acorn nut, locknut and washer (**Figure 19**).

4. Pull the arms and the washers off the pivot bolt.

5. Make a sketch indicating the order of parts removed so they may be installed in the same position.

6. Clean all parts except brake shoes in a solvent such as kerosene. Remove all traces of dirt, oil and grease.

7. Inspect each part for excessive wear and bends. Replace questionable parts or consider replacing the entire mechanism.

Removal/Installation

1. Loosen the cable anchor bolt holding the main cable (**Figure 10**).

2. Disconnect both ends of the short transverse cable from the brake arms (**Figure 9**).

3. Remove the mounting nut (**Figure 21**), washers and concave washers and pull the brake caliper off.

4. If replacing the caliper, take the old one to your dealer for an exact replacement.

5. Install by reversing these removal steps, noting the following.

6. Center the brakes so each brake shoe is the same distance from the rim before tightening the mounting nut (**Figure 17**).

7. Adjust the brake shoe position and cable length as described in Chapter Three.

5

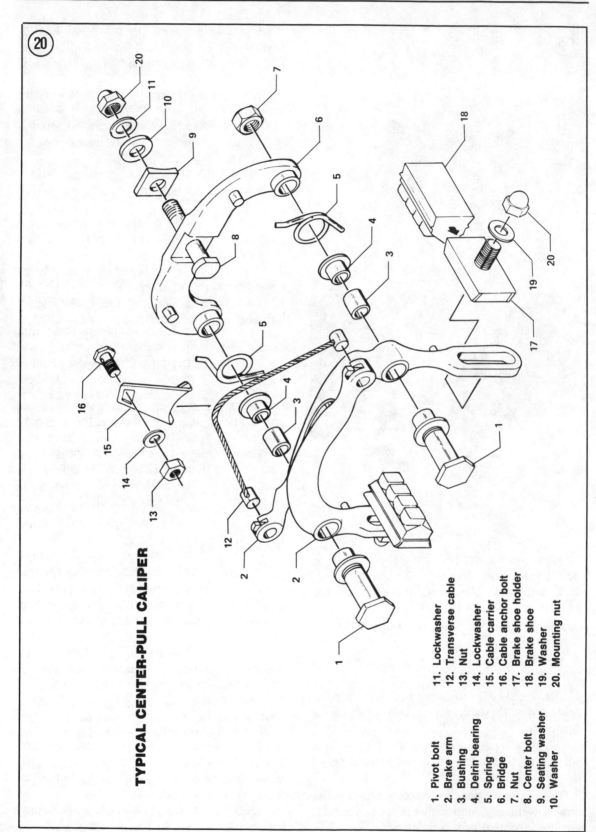

TYPICAL CENTER-PULL CALIPER

1. Pivot bolt
2. Brake arm
3. Bushing
4. Delrin bearing
5. Spring
6. Bridge
7. Nut
8. Center bolt
9. Seating washer
10. Washer
11. Lockwasher
12. Transverse cable
13. Nut
14. Lockwasher
15. Cable carrier
16. Cable anchor bolt
17. Brake shoe holder
18. Brake shoe
19. Washer
20. Mounting nut

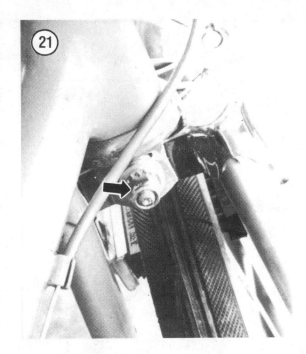

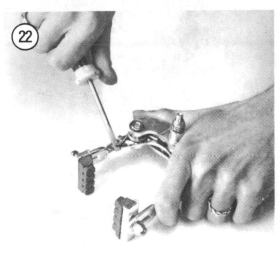

Overhaul

Replacement parts for calipers are very difficult to find. Before performing an overhaul, determine if parts are available. Unless you have a very expensive caliper brake assembly on your bicycle, it is usually cheaper to replace the entire assembly than to try to find replacement parts for it. Many bicycle dealers do not even carry replacement parts for most brakes.

If the caliper merely needs a good cleaning or if you have a source of replacement parts, use the following procedure.

1. Remove the caliper as described in this chapter.
2. Pry the spring ends (**Figure 22**) off the stops on the brake arms.
3. Remove both pivot bolts and the brake arms. Note the order of removal of any washers. Make a small sketch—don't rely on memory.
4. Remove the springs.

> *NOTE*
> *The springs are not interchangeable between the left- and right-hand side. Mark them with a piece of masking tape with an "R" and "L."*

5. Remove the brake shoes.
6. Clean all parts except the brake shoes in solvent such as kerosene. Remove all traces of dirt, oil and grease.
7. Inspect each part for excessive wear and bending. Make sure that the arms pivot smoothly on the pivot bolts. On some brakes, the arms pivot on small posts on the bridge; make certain the pivot action is smooth.
8. Place the springs on the bridge.

> *NOTE*
> *The left- and right-hand springs are not interchangeable. Refer to marks made in Step 4.*

9. Lightly oil the pivot bolt or bridge posts, all washers and the holes in the brake arms. Assemble the brake arms.
10. Assemble the brake arms on the bridge with the pivot bolts and washers. Refer to the sketch made in Step 3 or refer to **Figure 20**.
11. Pry the lower end of each spring over the stop on each brake arm with pliers.

> *WARNING*
> *Work carefully. If the spring slips, it can injure your fingers. Protect yourself accordingly.*

12. Install the transverse cable.
13. Mount the brake shoes, but do not tighten the nuts.
14. Install the brake caliper on the bicycle as described in this chapter.
15. Adjust the brakes as described in Chapter Three.

5

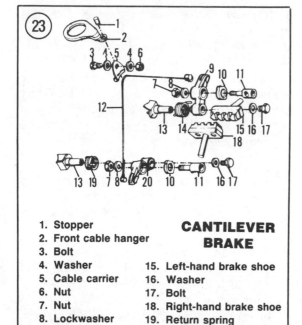

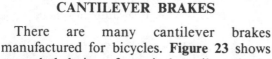

1. Stopper
2. Front cable hanger
3. Bolt
4. Washer
5. Cable carrier
6. Nut
7. Nut
8. Lockwasher
9. Brake arm
10. Adjust washer
11. Eye bolt
12. Center cable
13. Pivot shaft (brazed to frame)
14. Return spring

**CANTILEVER
BRAKE**

15. Left-hand brake shoe
16. Washer
17. Bolt
18. Right-hand brake shoe
19. Return spring
20. Brake arm

CANTILEVER BRAKES

There are many cantilever brakes manufactured for bicycles. **Figure 23** shows an exploded view of a typical cantilever brake caliper. If your caliper varies from this illustration, make a simple sketch of it as you disassemble it; most likely you will find it is built exactly like the one shown with the exception of a couple of small items.

Cantilever brakes are actually center-pull brakes that offer more leverage to gain better braking performance. The pivot bolts connect to pivot shafts that are brazed onto the fork or seat stays.

Removal/Installation

1. Loosen cable anchor bolt (**Figure 24**) holding the main cable.
2. Disconnect both ends of short transverse cable from each brake arm (A, **Figure 25**).
3. Unscrew each pivot bolt (B, **Figure 25**).
4. Pull the brake arms and spring off each pivot shaft.

5. Installation is the reverse of these steps, noting the following.
6. Make sure the return spring ends are indexed into the locating hole in each pivot shaft and brake arm.
7. Adjust the brake as described in Chapter Three.

Overhaul

There is really no disassembly procedure; the brake is totally disassembled during its removal from the fork or seat stays.

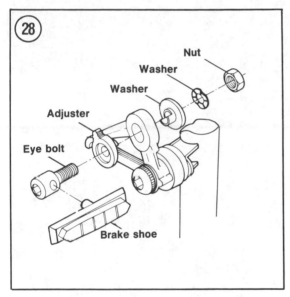

Replacement parts for calipers are very difficult to find. Unless you have a very expensive caliper brake assembly on your bicycle, it is usually cheaper to replace the entire assembly than to try to find replacement parts for it. Many bicycle dealers do not even carry replacement parts for most brakes.

BRAKE SHOES

The rubber pads on brake shoes can wear out or, through age or lack of use, harden. When this happens, replace all 4 brake shoes.

On some caliper assemblies, replacement rubber shoes are available separately. On some models the entire brake shoe assembly must be replaced. Even on models with replacement brake shoes it is suggested that the complete brake shoe assembly be replaced. It is a little more expensive but it is worth it, particularly if rust has damaged the threads on the old shoes.

If you are going to be doing a lot of cycling in hilly terrain where the brakes will be used a lot, consider buying brake shoes with an integral heat sink transfer block (**Figure 26**). They will help to keep the brakes a little cooler.

Brake shoes mount onto the calipers in different ways. On side-pull and center-pull models, the brake shoe has a threaded stud which fits through the caliper arm and is secured by a nut (**Figure 27**). On cantilever models, the brake shoes mount onto the calipers by an eye bolt and nut (**Figure 28**).

Replacement

1. On bicycles with quick-release levers, press the quick release mechanism to open the calipers as wide as possible (**Figure 29**).
2A. On side- and center-pull models, perform the following:
    a. Unscrew the nut holding the brake shoe assembly on the caliper (**Figure 27**).
    b. Remove the brake shoe assembly from the caliper.
    c. On models so equipped, slide the brake shoe out of the brake shoe holder.

d. On models so equipped, slide the new brake shoes back into the brake shoe holders.

e. Install the brake shoe assembly onto the caliper.

> *WARNING*
> *On models equipped with brake shoe holders, always install brake shoes and holders so the closed end of the metal holder faces forward (Figure 30). Otherwise, during braking the movement of the wheel will force the brake shoes out of the holders.*

2B. On cantilever models, perform the following:

a. Loosen the nut (**Figure 31**) on the eye bolt.

b. Slide the brake shoe assembly out of the eye bolt.

c. Install new brake shoe assemblies into the eye bolt.

3. Adjust the brakes as described in Chapter Three.

BRAKE TROUBLES

The following symptoms are common with caliper brake systems. For coaster brake troubleshooting, see Chapter Seven.

1. *Brakes stick*—Sticking can result from a bent hand lever or caliper part or a damaged cable housing. Check the following:

a. If the hand lever sticks, work the lever several times to see where the binding occurs. Often a lever will bind against the lever post. Insert a narrow-bladed screwdriver and gently pry them apart.

b. Make sure the cable runs smoothly in its housing and that the housing curves gradually without kinks or sharp bends. Remove the cable as described in this chapter, lubricate it and reinstall.

c. Calipers can stick because of bent parts or dirt accumulation. Clean the caliper and align parts carefully.

CAUTION
Cast aluminum parts break easily when bent; you will probably have to replace the caliper if it can't be straightened.

2. *Loose hand lever*—Tighten the hand lever on the handlebar as described in this chapter.

3. *One brake shoe drags on rim*—Be sure the caliper is centered when released (shoes are equal distance from rim) and the mounting nut is tight. Lubricate the pivot points of brake arms.

WARNING
Do not spill oil on brake shoes as it will make the brakes almost useless and the rubber with deteriorate.

4. *Main cable breaks frequently*—Check for points at which the cable may be chafing. Check the ends of the cable housing under the ferrules. If there is a burr on the end, file or cut it off. Check the housing for bends and kinks which may bind the cable and cause wear.

5. *Brakes slip excessively or squeal*—Check condition of brake shoes. If they are worn down or the rubber has hardened, replace them.

6. *Brakes shudder and act unevenly*—This is usually caused by loose brake components. Check tightness of caliper mounting nut (or bolt). Check and adjust the tightness of outer pivot bolt acorn nut on side-pull calipers.

5

DERAILLEUR POWER TRAIN

The power train on derailleur-equipped bicycles consists of one or more pedal-driven front sprockets linked to 2 or more rear sprockets via a chain (**Figure 1**).

On derailleur-equipped bicycles, derailleurs (from the French word meaning "to derail") move the chain to different sprockets when the shifter is moved. The number of rear sprockets and front sprockets determine how many gears or drive ratios are possible. For example:

a. 1 front sprocket, 5 rear sprockets = 5 speed.
b. 2 front sprockets, 5 rear sprockets = 10 speed.
c. 2 front sprockets, 6 rear sprockets = 15 speed.
d. 3 front sprockets, 6 rear sprockets = 18 speed.

The 18 speed is usually the maximum number of speeds available with the exception of some custom bicycles. For more than 18 speeds, the chain has to be very narrow and is therefore fragile.

The value of the drive ratio selected depends on the ratio between the number of teeth on the 2 sprockets in actual use. For example, with any given front sprocket, selecting a smaller rear sprocket (fewer teeth) raises the drive ratio to a higher gear.

Selecting a larger rear sprocket (more teeth) lowers the drive ratio to a lower gear. Changes in front sprocket size with any given rear sprocket have the opposite effect. That is, changing to a smaller front sprocket *lowers* the drive ratio to a lower gear; changing to a larger front sprocket *raises* the drive ratio to a higher gear. Gear ratios are discussed in detail in Chapter Twelve.

Table 1 is located at the end of this chapter.

PEDALS

Removal/Installation

A bent or broken pedal is very dangerous. Replace it immediately. Looking directly at the pedal that you are going to work on (**Figure 2**):

a. To loosen, turn the wrench toward the rear of the bicycle.
b. To tighten, turn the wrench toward the front of the bicycle.

NOTE
The left-hand pedal has left-hand threads so it will always be tightening while you are pedaling.

Take the defective pedal to your dealer. Carefully match threads with the new pedal to guarantee an exact replacement. Check the

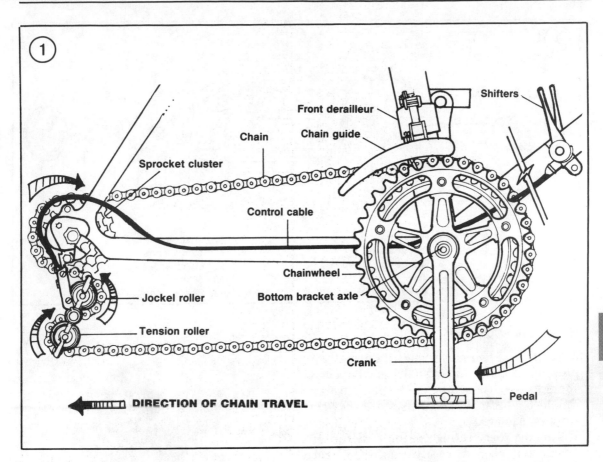

1

- Front derailleur
- Shifters
- Chain
- Chain guide
- Sprocket cluster
- Control cable
- Jockel roller
- Chainwheel
- Bottom bracket axle
- Tension roller
- Crank
- Pedal

DIRECTION OF CHAIN TRAVEL

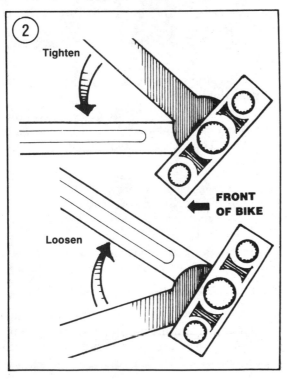

2

Tighten

FRONT
OF BIKE

Loosen

3

different pedal designs (**Figure 3**) that are available. You may want to change from the type that your bicycle presently has. The threaded portion must be the same diameter and have the same number of threads per inch.

Most pedals are marked as to which side of the bicycle they fit. Refer to **Table 1** for right- and left-hand markings.

6

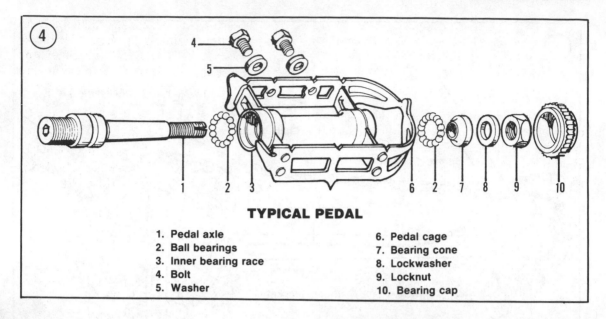

TYPICAL PEDAL

1. Pedal axle
2. Ball bearings
3. Inner bearing race
4. Bolt
5. Washer

6. Pedal cage
7. Bearing cone
8. Lockwasher
9. Locknut
10. Bearing cap

Disassembly/Assembly

Refer to **Figure 4** (typical) during this procedure. Only rat-trap (all metal) pedals should be disassembled. Rubber pedals should be discarded and replaced if they are worn or damaged.

1. Remove the bearing cap or dust cap by unscrewing it or gently prying it off, depending on type.

2. Hold axle assembly over a clean cloth. Remove the locknut (**Figure 5**), lockwasher and the bearing cone.

> *NOTE*
> *Many pedal assemblies have a different number of balls in the bearing on each end of the pedal.*

3. Remove the outer ball bearings. Count the number of balls in the bearing and write it down.

4. Pull the pedal axle from the pedal cage and remove the inner ball bearing. Count the number of balls in the bearing and write it down.

5. Clean all parts in solvent and thoroughly dry with compressed air.

6. Check that the pedal axle is straight and that the ball bearings and bearing cones are in good condition.

7. If any parts are worn or damaged, replace the entire pedal assembly. Parts may be available for some pedals but the price of a new set of pedals is not high.

8. Apply Lubriplate to the cup-shaped inner bearing race and install the ball bearings into the race. The grease should hold the balls into place.

> *NOTE*
> *After all the balls in place there should be enough room for one additional ball. This is correct; this space is intended for clearance.*

9. Insert the pedal axle into the pedal cage. Make sure that the axle goes in all the way and that the inner ball bearings are properly seated.

10. Apply Lubriplate to the cup-shaped outer bearing race and install the ball bearings into the race. The grease should hold the balls into place.

NOTE
After all the balls in place there should
be enough room for one additional ball.
This is correct; this space is intended for
clearance.

11. Screw on the bearing cone and tighten only finger-tight, then back it off about 1/4 turn. Install the lockwasher and the locknut. Hold the cone while tightening the locknut so that the cone will not be tightened.

12. Check that the pedal cage spins freely on its axle without binding or noise. If it binds, loosen the locknut, then loosen the cone about 1/2 turn. Retighten the locknut and check pedal again. Readjust the cone if necessary.

13. Check that there is no pedal side play on the axle (**Figure 6**). If any play is present, loosen the locknut, tighten the cone about 1/8 turn, then retighten the locknut. Check for side play again and readjust if necessary.

CRANKS

There are 3 types of cranks. The cottered crank has been used on most inexpensive bicycles in the past. It is still used on a few bicycles. The cranks are held onto the bottom bracket axle with a large bolt-like cotter pin (**Figure 7**). The majority of bicycles produced

today (even some relatively inexpensive ones) use a cotterless crank (**Figure 8**). These cranks are secured to the axle by a large bolt. Some bicycles (including many BMX racing bikes) use a one-piece crank and axle assembly (**Figure 9**).

This section includes procedures for cottered and cotterless cranks. One-piece cranks are covered under *1-piece Bottom Bracket Crankset* in this chapter.

Cottered Crank
Removal/Installation

Refer to **Figure 10** for this procedure.
1. If the right-hand crank is going to be removed, remove the chain as described in this chapter.
2. Make a cut-out in a hardwood block and mount the block in a vise (**Figure 11**).
3. Remove the nut (**Figure 7**) on the cotter pin.
4. Have an assistant help you lift the bicycle and rest the crank on the hardwood block. Align the crank so that the head of the cotter is over the cut-out (**Figure 11**).
5. Rap on the threaded end of the cotter pin with a plastic hammer. If you use a metal faced hammer, place a piece of hardwood on the cotter pin.

> *CAUTION*
> *Do not attempt this unless the crank is firmly supported on the hardwood block. If you pound on the cotter without support, the bottom bracket bearings and races will be damaged. In addition, do not hit the cotter directly with a metal faced hammer or the threaded end will be damaged.*

6. Remove the loosened cotter pin.
7. Pull the crank off the bottom bracket axle. The right-hand crank comes off complete with chainwheel.
8. Repeat Steps 3-7 for the other crank.
9. Check each crank for straightness by sighting down its length. If bent, replace it with an exact duplicate.
10. Slide the crank(s) onto the axle with the cotter hole opposite the slot in the axle.
11. Install the cotter pin with a washer and nut. Tighten the nut finger-tight. Install one

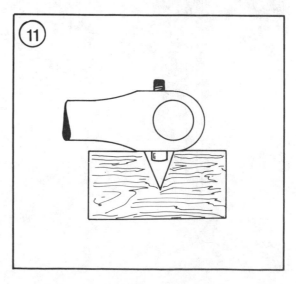

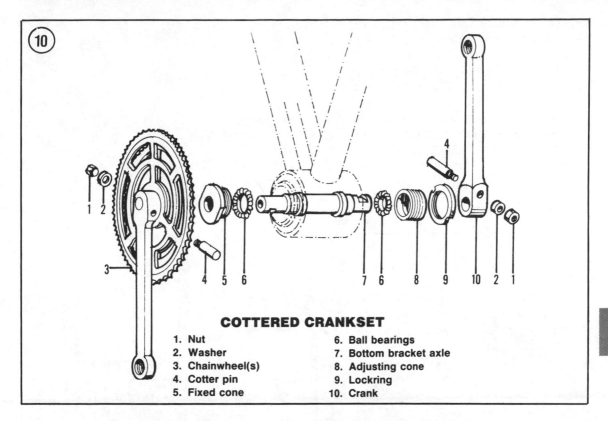

COTTERED CRANKSET

1. Nut
2. Washer
3. Chainwheel(s)
4. Cotter pin
5. Fixed cone
6. Ball bearings
7. Bottom bracket axle
8. Adjusting cone
9. Lockring
10. Crank

6

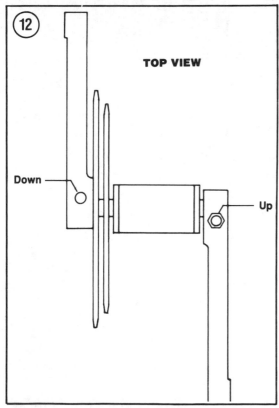

TOP VIEW

Down

Up

cotter facing up and one facing down (**Figure 12**).

12. Support the crank on the hardwood block as in Step 4 except put the threaded end of the cotter pin over the cut-out.

13. Drive the cotter pin in with a plastic mallet or a hammer and piece of hardwood.

14. Tighten the cotter nuts securely.

15. After about 50 miles, repeat Steps 12 through 14.

**Cotterless Crank
Removal/Installation**

Refer to **Figure 13** for this procedure.

This procedure requires special crank removal tools (**Figure 14**) designed specifically for each manufacturer's cranks or at least the thread design and diameter. These tools are available from most bicycle dealers. Have the dealer explain the use of the tools, since each tool is slightly different.

Cotterless cranks are usually made of dural aluminum rather than steel and are relatively soft. If treated properly they will last a long time, but they are easily damaged if

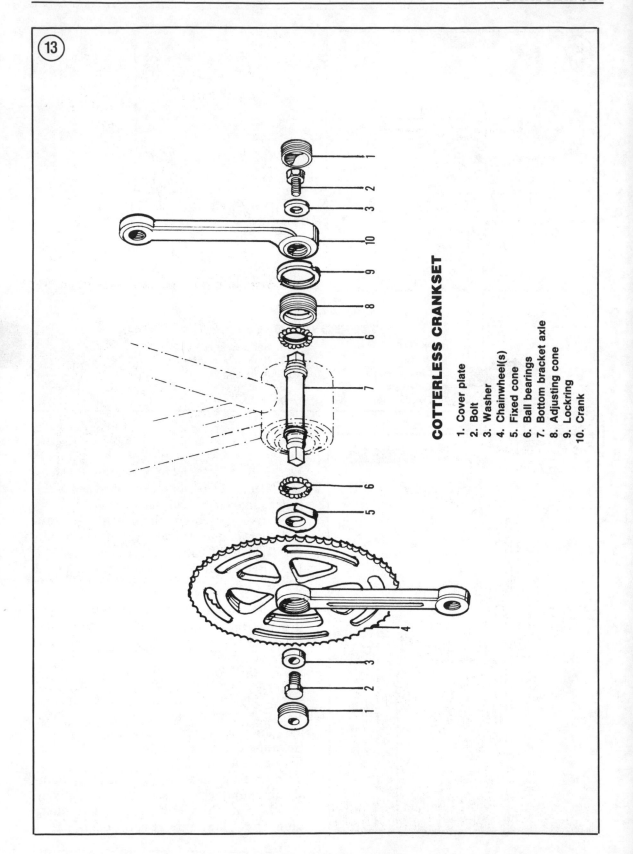

COTTERLESS CRANKSET

1. Cover plate
2. Bolt
3. Washer
4. Chainwheel(s)
5. Fixed cone
6. Ball bearings
7. Bottom bracket axle
8. Adjusting cone
9. Lockring
10. Crank

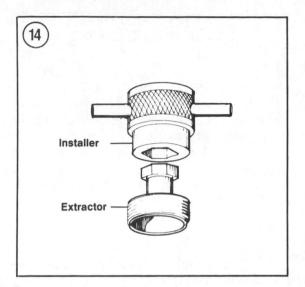

Installer

Extractor

6

mistreated. Do not remove cranks more often than necessary.

There are many different cranksets (**Figure 15**) available that may offer a feature that your present crankset does not. Check into these at a bicycle shop.

1. Remove the chain as described in this chapter if the right-hand crank is going to be removed.

2. Remove the crank arm cover (**Figure 16**) from the crank with an Allen wrench (or a special tool if necessary).

3. Using a correct size socket wrench, remove the bolt (**Figure 17**) securing the crank to the bottom bracket axle.

4. Screw the extractor portion (**Figure 18**) of the crankset tool into the dust cap threads.

CAUTION
Do not try to tighten the extractor
continuously until the crank comes off.
The threads inside the crank may strip.

5. Tighten the extractor portion and lightly tap on the end of it with a small hammer.

6. Repeat Step 5; continue tapping and tightening until the crank is pulled free from the bottom bracket axle.

7. To install a crank, lightly oil the crank bolt threads.

8. Align the crank 180° (opposite) from the crank on the other side and slide it on the bottom bracket axle.

9. Install the crank bolt finger-tight with the socket wrench.

10. Work the pedal slightly back and forth while tightening the crank bolt. Make sure it is tight or crank can slip and ruin both the crank and the axle.

11. Install the crank arm cover.

12. Repeat Steps 2-11 for the other side.

13. Install the chain if removed.

1-PIECE BOTTOM BRACKET CRANKSET

Disassembly

Refer to **Figure 19** for this procedure. Special bottom bracket tools (**Figure 20**) are required for this procedure. These tools are available from most bicycle dealers.

1. Remove both pedals as described in this chapter.

2. Using the correct size open-end wrench, remove the large locknut and lockwasher (**Figure 9**) on the left-hand side of bottom bracket.

3. Using the special tools, unscrew the adjusting cone (left-hand thread) and withdraw left-hand caged bearing.

4. Carefully maneuver and withdraw the chainwheel and the crank assembly out through the right-hand side of the bottom bracket.

5. Remove the right-hand caged bearing from the bottom bracket cup.

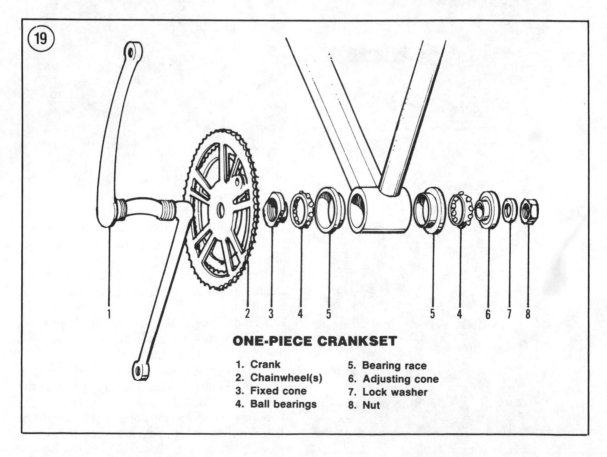

ONE-PIECE CRANKSET

1. Crank
2. Chainwheel(s)
3. Fixed cone
4. Ball bearings
5. Bearing race
6. Adjusting cone
7. Lock washer
8. Nut

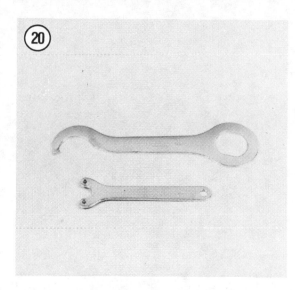

6. Remove the fixed cone and chain wheel from the crank assembly.

Inspection

1. Clean all parts in solvent and throughly dry with compressed air. Do not let the bearings spin while drying as they may be damaged.

2. Inspect the bearing cups in the bottom bracket. If they are worn or pitted, tap them out from the inside with a hardwood stick and a hammer (**Figure 21**). Take them to a bicycle dealer for exact replacement.

3. Inspect the caged ball bearings. If any balls are missing, worn or pitted or if the bearing retainer is cracked, replace the bearing with an exact replacement.

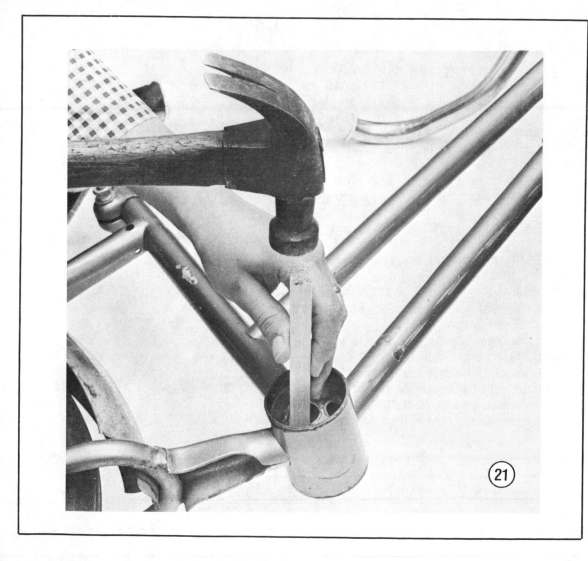

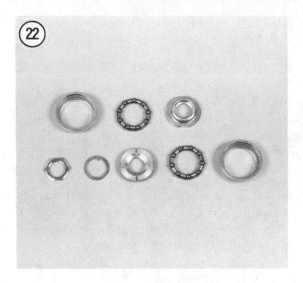

NOTE
*If the bearing cups and/or the caged bearings require replacement you should replace the entire assembly (**Figure 22**). BMX racers should consider replacing it with a sealed bearing set (**Figure 23**) for maximum dirt and moisture protection.*

4. Inspect the left-hand adjusting cone and right-hand fixed cone for wear or pitted. Replace if necessary.

5. Inspect the crank for cracks or fractures; replace if necessary. There are a lot of very strong aftermarket cranks available for BMX bikes (**Figure 24**). Check them out at a bicycle dealer.

6. Clean the inside of the bottom bracket thoroughly with solvent and dry with compressed air.

Assembly

1. If removed, tap new bottom bracket bearing cups into bottom bracket. Tap all around the perimeter of the cup lightly until the cup is completely seated in the frame bottom bracket.

2. Apply Lubriplate to the bearing cups in the frame bottom bracket.

3. Apply Lubriplate to the bearings. Work the grease into all recesses in the bearing retainer with your fingers.

4. Apply Lubriplate to left-hand adjusting cone.

5. Install the chainwheel onto the crank. Make sure the hole in the chainwheel is indexed onto the locating pin on the crank.

6. Install the right-hand fixed cone onto the crank and tighten securely.

7. Install the right-hand caged bearing into the cup in the bottom bracket.

8. Insert the left-hand crank and chainwheel through the right-hand side of the bottom bracket. Work it around carefully until the crank fits correctly into the bottom bracket.

CAUTION
Check that the right-hand bearing fits properly against the right-hand fixed cone and the cup in the bottom bracket.

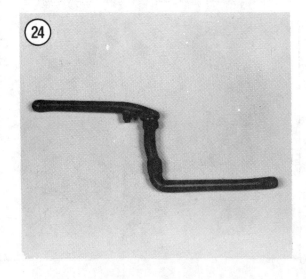

9. Slide the left-hand caged bearing over the left-hand crank and fit it into the bearing cup.

10. Slide the adjusting cone over the left-hand crank and fit it into the caged bearing.

11. Push on the crank assembly from the right-hand side and make sure it is properly seated.

12. Screw the adjusting cone on finger-tight. Back it off about 1/4 turn.

13. Install the lockwasher and the locknut. Tighten the locknut.

14. Install the left-hand pedal.

15. Holding a crank in each hand, try to move the crank assembly from side to side. If there is any play, loosen the locknut, tighten the adjustable bearing cone about 1/8 turn, then retighten the locknut. Check again and readjust if necessary until there is no side play.

16. Check that the cranks spin freely without binding or noise. If there is any binding, loosen the locknut, loosen the adjustable bearing cone about 1/8 turn, then tighten the locknut. Check crank freedom again and readjust if necessary. If noise is present, chances are the crankset was not lubricated or assembled properly. Disassemble and correct the situation, checking for damaged parts or dirt.

3-PIECE BOTTOM BRACKET CRANKSET

Disassembly

Refer to **Figure 11** or **Figure 13** for this procedure.

1. Remove the cottered or cotterless cranks as described in this chapter.

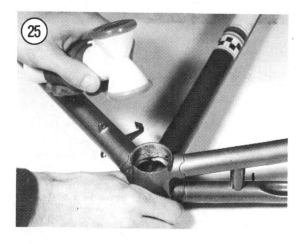

NOTE
The lockrings on some models have a left-hand thread.

2. Using the special tool shown in **Figure 14** or **Figure 20**, remove the lockring.

3. Loosen the adjusting cone.

4. Lean the bicycle to the left and place a clean cloth under the bottom bracket.

5. Hold the right-hand end of axle tightly against bottom bracket. Remove the adjusting cone and the loose ball bearings. Count the number of ball bearings and write it down so that the same number will be reinstalled later.

NOTE
Some cranksets have caged bearings. Simply remove the caged bearing after removing the adjusting cone.

6. Pull the axle out of the left side of the bottom bracket.

7. Remove the ball bearings from the fixed cup on the right-hand side. Do not remove fixed cup from the frame. Refer to *Inspection* Step 4.

Inspection

1. Check inside bottom bracket shell for a plastic liner. Remove it if present.

2. Clean all parts in solvent and thoroughly dry with compressed air.

3. Clean the inside of the bottom bracket shell in frame with solvent and thoroughly dry with compressed air.

4. Inspect the bearing surfaces on fixed cup. Use a flashlight if necessary (**Figure 25**). If the fixed cup is worn or pitted, take the bicycle to a bicycle dealer for replacement; this is a delicate job requiring experience.

5. Inspect the bearing surfaces on the axle and the adjusting cone. If worn or pitted, they must be replaced. Take the old parts to a bicycle dealer for exact replacements.

6. Inspect the ball bearings. Check balls for wear or pitting. If bearings are caged, check that no balls are missing and that the retainer is not bent or cracked. Replace bearings, if necessary. Take the old bearings to a bicycle dealer for exact replacement.

6

NOTE
If the bearing cups, the ball bearings (or caged bearings) or the axle require replacement you should replace the entire assembly.

Assembly

1. Lay the bicycle on its right-hand side. Apply Lubriplate to inside bearing surface of fixed cup.

2A. Install the bearings into the fixed cup. Be sure to install the same number of balls as noted in during removal.

2B. If the bearings are caged, work Lubriplate into all recesses on the retainer before installing. Install the caged bearing assembly.

3. Insert the chainwheel end (long end) into the bottom bracket and through the fixed cup. Be careful not to disturb the ball bearings in the fixed hub.

4. Install the plastic liner in the bottom bracket if it was removed.

5. Apply Lubriplate to bearing surface of adjusting cup.

6A. Install the same number of balls as noted during removal. Add a layer of Lubriplate over the balls. The grease will hold them in place.

6B. If the bearings are caged, work Lubriplate into all recesses on the retainer before installing. Install the caged bearing assembly.

7. Hold the axle firmly against fixed cup to keep bearings in place.

8. Tilt the bicycle over on its left-hand side and screw the adjusting cup onto the bottom bracket.

9. Tighten the adjusting cup only finger-tight, then back it off about 1/4 turn. Install the lockring and tighten with the special tools.

10. Holding each end of the axle, try to move it from side to side. If you feel any play, loosen the lockring, tighten adjustable cup about 1/8 turn. Retighten the lockring. Check again and readjust if necessary until there is no side play.

11. Check that the axle spins freely without binding or noises. If there is any binding, loosen the lockring, loosen the adjustable cup 1/8 turn and retighten the lockring. Check again and readjust if necessary. If noise is present, chances are the crankset was not

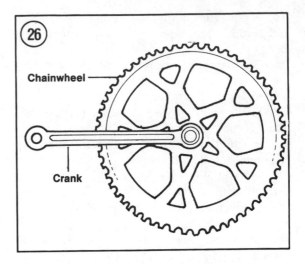

lubricated or assembled properly. Disassemble and repeat assembly procedure. Check for damaged parts and dirt.

CHAINWHEEL (FRONT SPROCKET)

1-Piece Crankset
Removal/Installation

On some 1-piece cranksets, the chainwheel (front sprocket) is permanently mounted on the crank (**Figure 26**). Remove and replace entire crankset as described in this chapter.

Some 1-piece cranksets have a separate chainwheel. To remove the chain wheel, remove the 1-piece crankset assembly as described in this chapter. Remove and replace the chainwheel.

Bolted Front Chainwheel
Removal/Installation

Refer to **Figure 27** for this procedure.

1. Remove the chain as described in this chapter.

NOTE
On models with 2 front chainwheels, one chainwheel is attached to the front of the crank and the other is attached to the rear. They share one common set of nuts and bolts.

2. Remove bolts and nuts (**Figure 28**) securing the chainwheel(s) to the cranks.

3. Take the old chainwheel(s) to a bicycle dealer and get exact replacements.

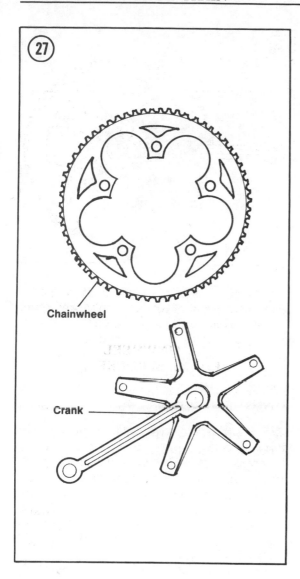

Chainwheel

Crank

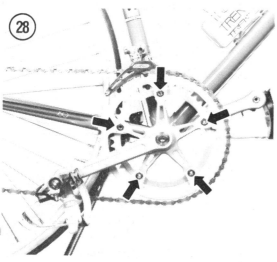

NOTE
*If you want to change the gearing on your bicycle, now is the time to do so. If you want to be higher geared, get a chainwheel with more teeth; if you want to be lower geared, get one with fewer teeth (**Figure 29**). See Chapter Twelve for gearing information.*

4. Fit the new sprocket(s) in place. Install all bolts and nuts only finger-tight.

5. Tighten each bolt about 1/2 turn, working around the sprocket until all bolts are tight. If you tighten one bolt completely while the rest are still loose, you may warp the sprocket(s) and have to replace it again.

CHAIN
Removal/Installation

1. Select any link on the chain and insert it in the chain rivet remover (**Figure 30**).

NOTE
***Figure 30** is shown with the chain already removed from the bicycle for clarity.*

6

2. Screw the driving point in until it touches a chain rivet.

3. Screw the driving point against the rivet and drive it out. *Do not* drive the rivet all the way out of the rear side plate.

4. Back the driving point out of the link.

5. Remove the chain from the chain wheel and the rear sprocket and derailleur mechanism.

6. Clean and lubricate the chain as described in Chapter Three.

7. If installing a new chain, measure it against the old chain. If necessary, use the chain tool and remove any links so the new chain is the same length as the original chain.

8. Install the chain around the chainwheel, the rear sprocket and the deraileur. Refer to **Figure 1** to be sure it is routed correctly.

9. Place the ends of the chain together and use the chain tool to install rivet. Make sure that the rivet extends the same distance from each link.

Chain Repair

The chain must be repaired when a link becomes too tight or too loose.

If a link is too tight due to bent side plates, replace the link. If the side plates are not bent, apply penetrating oil liberally to the link and flex it several times. If the link is still too tight, replace it.

1. Remove the chain as described in this chapter.

2. Insert the defective link in the chain rivet remover (**Figure 30**).

3. Screw the driving point against one of the rivets and drive it out. *Do not* drive it all the way out of the rear side plate.

4. Repeat Step 2 for rivet on other end of defective link.

5. Insert the chain end in tool with the rivet *toward* the driving point.

6. Insert the new link in the tool and drive the rivet in.

7. Install the chain as described in this chapter.

Chain Tension Adjustment

Proper chain tension is important. If the tension is too loose, the chain may skip while

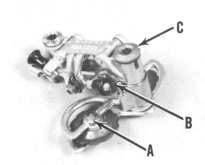

pedaling, particularly in high gear where pedaling effort is the highest. If the tension is too tight, pedaling effort and chain wear increase. Use as little chain tension as possible. The method of adjustment varies according to type of bicycle. These adjustment procedures are for the most common derailleurs used. There may be some slight variation with the multitude of derailleurs in use today.

Campagnolo

1. Remove the tension roller bolt (A, **Figure 31**) and the tension roller. Remove the chain from the cage.

2. Remove the cage stop bolt (B, **Figure 31**) and let the cage unwind completely.

3. Remove the cage pivot bolt (C, **Figure 31**) with an Allen wrench and remove the cage.

4. Note carefully which cage hole the spring engaged before completely removing the cage.

5. Reinstall the cage with the spring end engaged in the next hole *counterclockwise* from the previously used hole.

6. Reinstall and tighten the cage pivot bolt.

7. Wind the cage *counterclockwise* 1 turn, hold in this position and reinstall the cage stop bolt.

8. Install the tension roller and tension roller bolt.

Install the chain onto the cage.

9. Road test the bicycle.

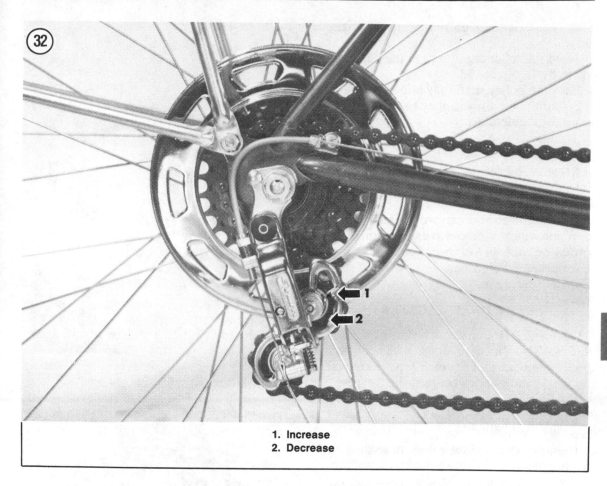

1. Increase
2. Decrease

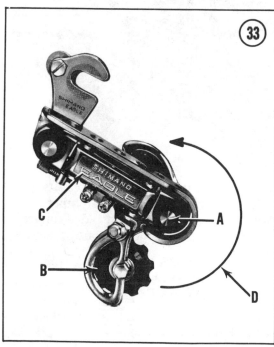

10. Readjust if necessary by removing the stop bolt. Wind the cage *counterclockwise* 1/2 turn to decrease tension.

Huret

Move the tension spring to a higher notch to increase tension or to a lower notch to decrease tension (**Figure 32**).

Shimano

1. Remove derailleur as described in this chapter.
2. Pry off the roller spring cap (A, **Figure 33**) and remove the circlip.
3. Remove the roller assembly (B, **Figure 33**) from the main body (C, **Figure 33**). Replace the spring with a new one.
4. Slide the roller shaft into the main body so that the spring is seated in the hole in the

roller cage but the stop pin clears the main body.

5. Wind the roller cage 1 turn in the direction shown by D, **Figure 33**.
6. Push the pulley shaft fully into main body.
7. Install the circlip and the cap.
8. Install the derailleur.

Sun Tour

1. Remove the chain from the chain cage. Note that it is not necessary to remove the tension roller.
2. Hold the cage and remove the stop bolt.
3. Wind the cage *clockwise* to increase tension or *counterclockwise* to decrease it.
4. Reinstall the stop bolt.
5. Install the chain.

FREEWHEEL CLUSTER

The inside of a freewheel cluster is built one of 2 ways—splined or notched. There is a special removal tool for each type. Removal and installation varies between the 2 types.

**Splined Freewheel Cluster
Removal/Installation**

1. Remove the rear wheel as described in Chapter Four.
2. On quick-release hubs, unscrew the adjusting nut.
3. Remove the mounting stud along with the lever and the springs (**Figure 34**).
4. Clamp the hub in a vise with soft jaws. Position the hub with the freewheel cluster facing up.
5. Remove the spacer nut from hub (inside freewheel cluster) with a cone wrench.

NOTE
*Some hubs use a spacer with a locknut.
If so equipped, remove locknut first.*

6. Remove the hub from the vise.
7. Clamp the freewheel removal tool in the vise.
8. Guide the hub onto the tool so that freewheel splines and tool align (**Figure 35**).
9. Rotate the wheel *counterclockwise* until the hub comes off the freewheel.
10. If so equipped, remove the spoke protector and the spacer washer.

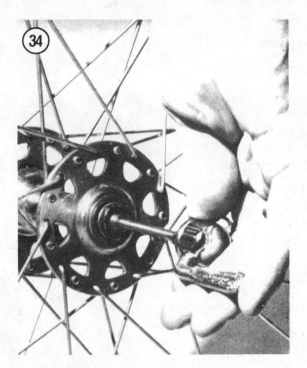

11. Install by reversing these removal steps. Apply a liberal coat of high-temperature grease to hub sprockets and threaded surfaces of the freewheel cluster body before installation.

**Notched Freewheel Cluster
Removal/Installation**

1. Remove the rear wheel as described in Chapter Four.

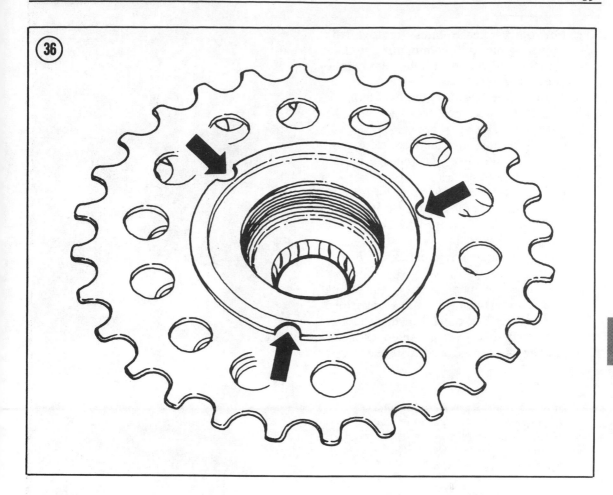

2. On quick-release hubs, unscrew the adjusting nut.

3. Remove the mounting stud with the lever and the springs (**Figure 34**).

4. Clamp the hub in a vise with soft jaws.

5. Position the hub with the freewheel cluster facing up.

6. Remove the spacer nut from the hub (inside freewheel cluster) with a cone wrench.

NOTE
Some hubs use a spacer with a locknut.
If so equipped, remove the locknut first.

7. Remove the hub from the vise.

8A. On quick-release hubs, perform the following:

   a. Install the mounting stud in the hub.
   b. Slide the freewheel removal tool over the mounting stud and make sure that the lugs engage in the notches on the cluster body.

   c. Install and fully tighten the adjusting nut on the end of the mounting stud to hold the tool in place.

8B. On standard mounted hubs, perform the following:

   a. Slide the freewheel tool over the axle and engage the tool lugs with the cluster body notches.
   b. Install the axle mounting nut and tighten fully to hold the tool in place.

9A. If the notches (**Figure 36**) in the freewheel cluster are in good condition, proceed with the following:

   a. Clamp the flats of freewheel removal tool in a vise.
   b. Install the wheel and hub with cluster resting on top of vise (**Figure 37**).
   c. Turn the wheel *counterclockwise* to loosen the cluster.
   d. Remove the wheel assembly from the vise.

e. On quick-release hubs, remove the adjusting nut and the mounting stud.

f. On standard mounted hubs, remove the mounting nut.

g. Remove the freewheel removal tool.

h. Clamp the freewheel tool back into the vise.

i. Guide the hub onto the frewheel tool so that the freewheel lugs engage in the cluster body notches.

j. Rotate the wheel *counterclockwise* until the hub comes off the freewheel.

9B. If the notches in the freewheel cluster are damaged, proceed as follows:

a. Clamp a large screw extractor (**Figure 38**) in a vise.

b. Remove the axle assembly (including the bearings) from the hub as described under *Hub Disassembly* in this chapter.

c. Guide the hub over the screw extractor and engage the extractor with the cluster body.

NOTE
If the tip of the screw extractor contacts the opposite side of the hub preventing the extractor from firmly gripping the cluster body, grind 1/4 in. (6.5 mm) from the tip of the extractor.

WARNING
When using a grinder, wear a face shield or safety goggles to protect your eyes. The metal in a screw extractor is very hard.

d. Rotate the wheel *counterclockwise* and loosen the freewheel cluster. Continue turning the wheel until the hub comes off the freewheel cluster.

e. Place the freewheel cluster over the vise jaws.

f. From the opposite side of the hub, pound the screw extractor out with a hammer and punch.

10. If so equipped, remove the spoke protector and the spacer washer.

11. If working on a freewheel with damaged notches, perform the following prior to reassembly:

a. Overhaul the freewheel as described in this chapter. The damaged portion of the freewheel must be replaced.

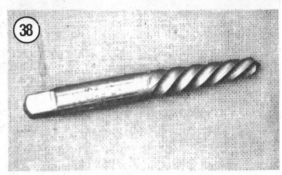

b. Reassemble the axle assembly in the hub as described in this chapter.

12. Install by reversing the removal steps. Apply a liberal coat of high-temperature grease to hub, sprockets and threaded surfaces of freewheel cluster body before installation.

Disassembly

Refer to **Figure 39** for this procedure. Special tools called cog or rear sprocket removal tools (**Figure 40**) are required for sprocket removal. These tools are available from most bicycle dealers.

1. Hold the right-hand side of sprocket No. 3 with one sprocket tool.

2. Hold the left-hand side of sprocket No. 1 with other sprocket tool (**Figure 41**).

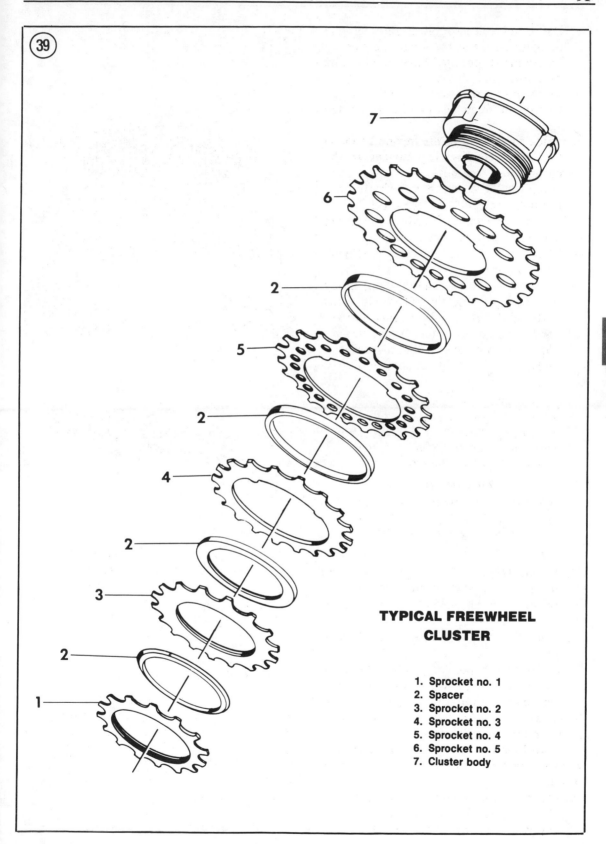

TYPICAL FREEWHEEL CLUSTER

1. Sprocket no. 1
2. Spacer
3. Sprocket no. 2
4. Sprocket no. 3
5. Sprocket no. 4
6. Sprocket no. 5
7. Cluster body

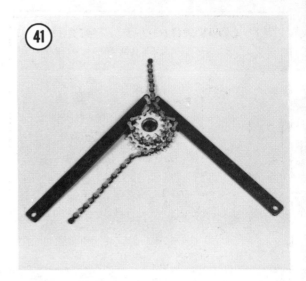

3. Rotate sprocket No. 1 *counterclockwise* and loosen it. Remove sprocket No. 1.
4. Hold the right-hand side of sprocket No. 3.
5. Hold the left-hand side of sprocket No. 2. Rotate sprocket No. 2 *counterclockwise* to loosen it. Remove sprocket No. 2.
6. Slide off sprockets No. 3, No. 4 and No. 5 and the spacers in between each sprocket from the cluster body.

Inspection

The price of a new cluster assembly (**Figure 42**) is relatively low today. If any of the components show damage in the following inspection, it is suggested that you replace the entire assembly. That way you will not have a new part trying to work with an assortment of older parts that have already taken a wear pattern.
1. Clean all parts in solvent and thoroughly dry.
2. Inspect sprockets No. 1 and No. 2 for stripped threads.
3. Inspect all sprockets for damaged, bent or worn teeth.
4. Inspect the cluster body for stripped or damaged threads.

Assembly

1. Onto the cluster body, install sprocket No. 5, a spacer, sprocket No. 4, a spacer, sprocket No. 3 and a spacer.

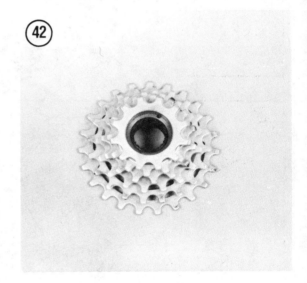

2. Screw sprocket No. 2 *clockwise* onto the cluster body. Tighten finger-tight.
3. Hold the left-hand side of sprocket No. 3 with a sprocket tool.
4. Hold the right-hand side of sprocket No. 2 with a sprocket tool and tighten fully *clockwise*.
5. Install a spacer, then screw on sprocket No. 1 *clockwise*.
6. Hold the left-hand side of sprocket No. 3 with a sprocket tool.
7. Hold the right-hand side of sprocket No. 1 with a sprocket tool and tighten fully *clockwise*.
8. Install freewheel cluster as described in this chapter.

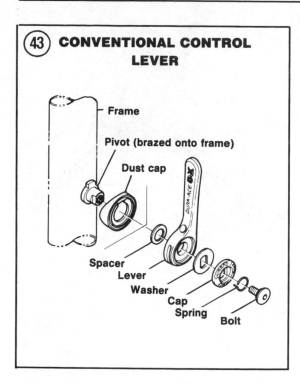

43 CONVENTIONAL CONTROL LEVER

- Frame
- Pivot (brazed onto frame)
- Dust cap
- Spacer
- Lever
- Washer
- Cap
- Spring
- Bolt

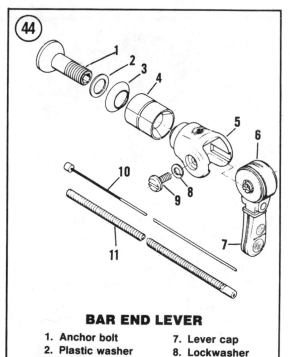

44

BAR END LEVER

1. Anchor bolt	7. Lever cap
2. Plastic washer	8. Lockwasher
3. Tapered washer	9. Mounting bolt
4. Segment	10. Inner cable
5. Body	11. Outer casing
6. Lever assembly	

CONTROL LEVERS AND CABLES

Conventional Control Levers

Control levers for derailleurs are very simple. Most control levers are mounted onto brazed-on lugs on the frame (**Figure 43**).

To disassemble, unscrew the screw or adjustable bolt and slide all of the parts off the stud. Sketch the order of disassembly so that all parts may be reassembled properly.

Clean all parts in solvent and wipe with a clean dry cloth. Rust or corrosion may be removed with fine steel wool or crocus cloth. If many of the parts are rusted, corroded or bent it is suggested that the entire assembly be replaced. They are not expensive; also, many dealers do not carry replacement parts for control levers.

Reassemble, noting order of parts sketched during removal. Do not lubricate control lever parts.

Bar End Control Levers

Bar end control levers are simple and virtually trouble-free (**Figure 44**).

To disassemble the lever, perform the following:

a. Remove the cable as described under *Cable Replacement* in this chapter.
b. Remove the lever mounting screw.
c. Remove the lever from the body.
d. To remove the body from the handlebar, loosen the hex bolt with an Allen wrench and pull the body out.
e. Assemble by reversing these disassembly steps.

Cable Replacement

1. Loosen the cable anchor bolt at the derailleur.
2. Disconnect the cable from the control lever.
3. Take the old cable to a bicycle dealer.
4. Select a new cable at least as long as the old one or longer. Never buy one that is shorter. Make sure the control lever end of the cable is the same shape.
5. Carefully examine the cable housing. Check for kinks or bends, particularly at the ferrules.

6

6. If the ends of the cable housing are damaged, perform the following:

   a. Cut the ends off cleanly.

   b. Cut through the outer covering with a knife.

   c. Using wire cutters, cut the end of the housing off between the coils. Do not leave a burr, as it will eventually cut into your cable. Either snip or file it off.

7. If the cable housing is damaged, replace it. Purchase a length of cable housing slightly longer than the original; you can always cut it shorter to fit. Make sure that your ferrules fit the new housing; if not, purchase new ferrules to fit.

8. Grease the cable lightly with Lubriplate and thread it through the cable housing. Continually twist the cable *counterclockwise* while threading it in order to keep the cable end from unraveling.

9. Connect the cable to the control lever. Hold tension on the derailleur end of the cable. Work the control lever back and forth and make sure the cable and lever work smoothly.

10. Thread the cable end into the derailleur cable anchor bolt. Do not trim the cable at this time.

11. Adjust the derailleur as described in Chapter Three.

12. Cut off excess cable *after* adjusting the derailleur.

FRONT DERAILLEUR

Removal/Installation

1. Remove the screw (A, **Figure 45**), nut and spacer on the end of the chain guide.

2. Loosen the cable anchor bolt (B, **Figure 45**) on the derailleur and pull the cable out.

3. Remove screw(s) (**Figure 46**) clamping the derailleur to the frame and remove the derailleur.

4. When installing the derailleur, secure it to frame with clamp screw(s) so that the bottom of the chain guide is about 3/16 in. (5 mm) above the teeth on the largest sprocket (**Figure 47**).

5. Align the chain guide parallel to the sprockets by turning the derailleur on the seat tube. Tighten the clamp screw(s).

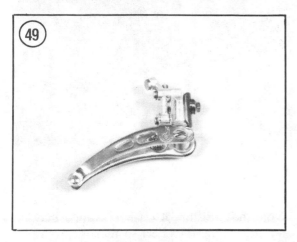

6. Move the chain up into the derailleur, above the place where the spacer is going to be installed.

7. Install the spacer at the end of the chain guide. Secure the spacer with the screw and nut.

NOTE
*Make sure that the chain goes through the chain guide and over the spacer (**Figure 48**).*

8. Thread the cable through the cable anchor bolt.

9. Adjust the derailleur as described in Chapter Three.

Overhaul

Front derailleurs (**Figure 49**) are simple devices requiring little more than occasional adjustment and cleaning. Overhaul is rarely required. In most cases, replacement of the entire derailleur is less expensive than an overhaul.

Figure 50 shows a typical front derailleur. Take the defective derailleur to a bicycle

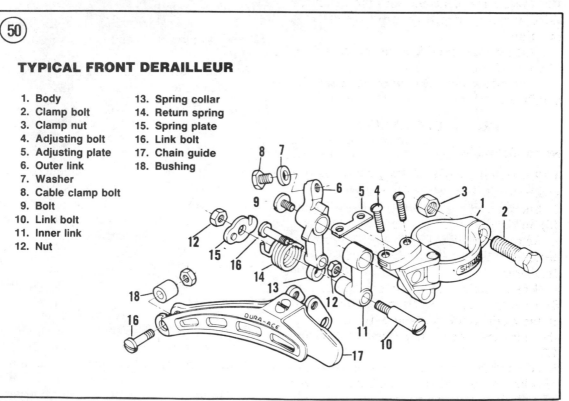

TYPICAL FRONT DERAILLEUR

1. Body
2. Clamp bolt
3. Clamp nut
4. Adjusting bolt
5. Adjusting plate
6. Outer link
7. Washer
8. Cable clamp bolt
9. Bolt
10. Link bolt
11. Inner link
12. Nut
13. Spring collar
14. Return spring
15. Spring plate
16. Link bolt
17. Chain guide
18. Bushing

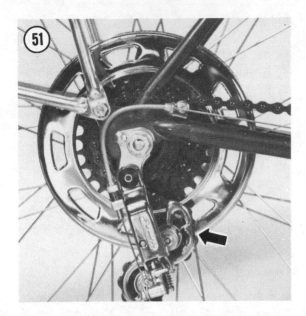

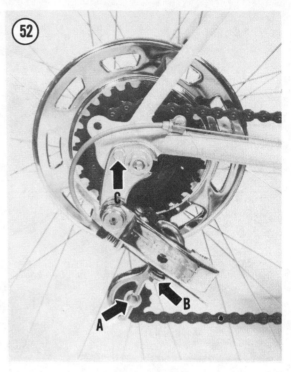

dealer for replacement. They might be able to suggest substitutes if they do not have the exact assembly you need.

REAR DERAILLEUR

Removal

1. Have an assistant hold the rear wheel off the ground.

CAUTION
Shift gears only while rear wheel and pedals are in motion or the derailleur may be damaged.

2. Rotate the pedals in a forward motion and move the rear derailleur shifter all the way forward. This will shift the chain onto the small sprocket of the rear freewheel.
3. Remove the rear wheel as described in Chapter Four.
3A. On derailleurs such as the Huret Allvit and Schwinn GT-200, pry the chain tension spring from its seat to relieve all tension (**Figure 51**).
3B. On all other derailleurs, remove the chain from the front chainwheel.
4A. On Sun Tour GT, remove the chain from the tension roller. It is not necessary to disassemble tension roller on this derailleur.
4B. On all other derailleurs, remove the bolt securing the tension roller (A, **Figure 52**).

Note the position of washers (which may be on either side of roller) so that they may be reinstalled properly.
5. Loosen the cable anchor bolt (B, **Figure 52**) and pull the cable and housing free of the derailleur.
6. Loosen the mounting bolt (C, **Figure 52**) and remove the derailleur assembly.

Installation

1. Correctly position the derailleur on the frame and install the mounting bolt.
2. If installing a new derailleur (except Sun Tour), remove the bolt securing the tension roller and remove the tension roller.
3. Install the rear wheel as described in Chapter Four.
4. Make sure that the chain is on smallest rear sprocket.
5. Loop the chain in front of jockey roller and toward the rear so that it will pass over the top of the tension roller (**Figure 53**).
6. If removed, mount the tension roller in the derailleur cage so that the chain passes over and behind it (**Figure 54**). Be sure all parts

required. In most cases, replacement of the entire derailleur is less expensive than an overhaul.

Figure 56 shows a typical rear derailleur. Take the defective derailleur to a bicycle dealer for replacement. They might be able to suggest substitutes if they do not have the exact assembly you need.

HUBS

This section describes front and rear hubs except multi-speed and coaster brake hubs. Multi-speed and coaster brake hubs are described in Chapter Seven.

Front hubs on all bicycles and rear hubs on derailleur-equipped bicycles are very similar. These consist of an axle, bearings, cones and the hub shell. **Figure 57** shows a typical hub. The cones are adjustable to eliminate excessive wheel play on the axle.

There are many exotic lightweight hubs (**Figure 58**) available from bicycle dealers. Prior to replacing some of the components on your hub, check the possibility of replacing the hub with a newer one. They are not very expensive.

Cone Adjustment

Examine the hub on your bicycle. If the cone has a thin locknut in addition to the nut holding the wheel to the fork or frame, as shown in **Figure 59**, use the first procedure. If

removed in Step 4B are installed in their proper positions.

7. Adjust the derailleur as described in Chapter Three.

8. Adjust the chain tension as described in this chapter.

Overhaul

Rear derailleurs (**Figure 55**) are simple devices requiring little more than occasional adjustment and cleaning. Overhaul is rarely

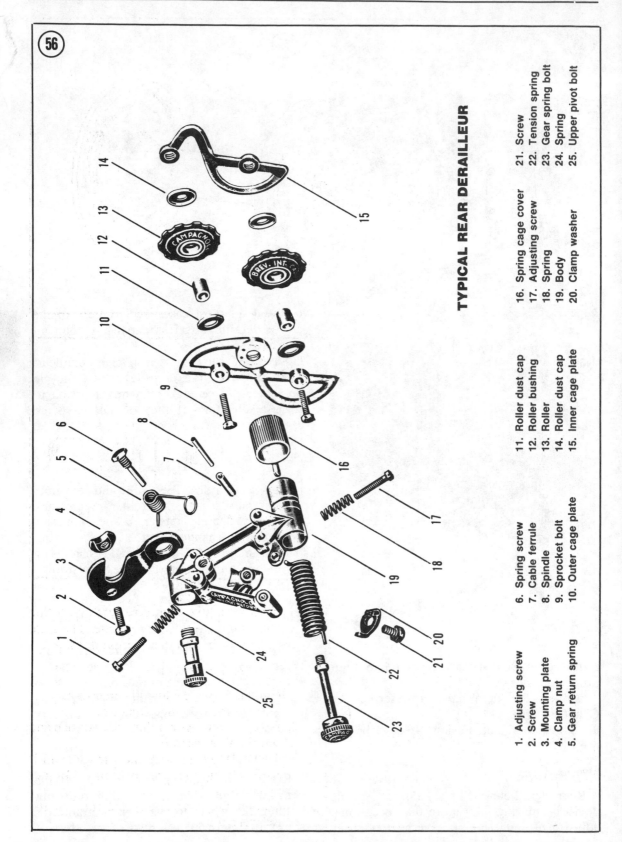

TYPICAL REAR DERAILLEUR

1. Adjusting screw
2. Screw
3. Mounting plate
4. Clamp nut
5. Gear return spring
6. Spring screw
7. Cable ferrule
8. Spindle
9. Sprocket bolt
10. Outer cage plate
11. Roller dust cap
12. Roller bushing
13. Roller
14. Roller dust cap
15. Inner cage plate
16. Spring cage cover
17. Adjusting screw
18. Spring
19. Body
20. Clamp washer
21. Screw
22. Tension spring
23. Gear spring bolt
24. Spring
25. Upper pivot bolt

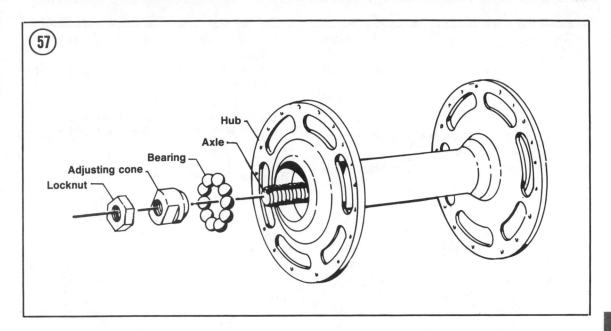

Figure 57 — Hub, Axle, Bearing, Adjusting cone, Locknut

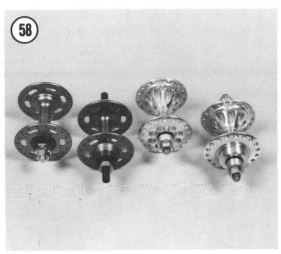

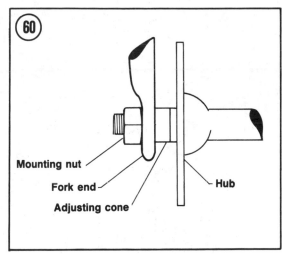

Figure 60 — Mounting nut, Fork end, Adjusting cone, Hub

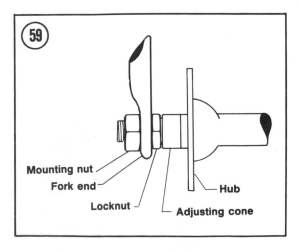

Figure 59 — Mounting nut, Fork end, Locknut, Hub, Adjusting cone

the hub looks like **Figure 60**, without a thin locknut, use the second procedure. The third procedure is for all quick-release hubs.

Hubs with thin locknut

Refer to **Figure 59** for this procedure.
1. Loosen one axle mounting nut.
2. Hold the cone with a thin cone wrench and loosen the thin locknut.
3. Tighten the cone with the wrench until it seats firmly against the bearings. Do not over-tighten.
4. Loosen the cone about 1/2 turn so the wheel turns freely.

5. Hold the cone in this position with the wrench and tighten the thin locknut against the cone.

6. Center the wheel in the fork or frame and tighten the axle mounting nut.

Hubs without thin locknut

Refer to **Figure 60** for this procedure.

1. Loosen one axle mounting nut.

2. Tighten the cone with the wrench until it seats firmly against the bearings. Do not over-tighten.

3. Loosen the cone about 1/2 turn so the wheel turns freely.

4. Hold cone in this position, center the wheel in the fork or frame and tighten the axle mounting nut.

Hubs with quick-release

1. Unlock the lever and remove the wheel.

2. Hold the cone with a thin cone wrench and loosen the thin locknut.

3. Tighten the cone with the wrench until it seats firmly against the bearings. Do not over-tighten.

4. Loosen the cone about 1/2 turn so the wheel turns freely.

5. Hold cone in this position with the wrench and tighten the thin locknut against the cone.

6. Install the wheel as described in Chapter Four.

Disassembly

Refer to **Figure 61** for a typical front hub and to **Figure 62** for a typical rear hub.

All steps relate to both the front and rear hub unless otherwise specified.

1. Mount the bicycle in a repair stand and remove the wheel as described in Chapter Four.

2. On quick-release hubs, perform the following:

    a. Hold the lever firmly and remove the adjusting nut and tension spring.

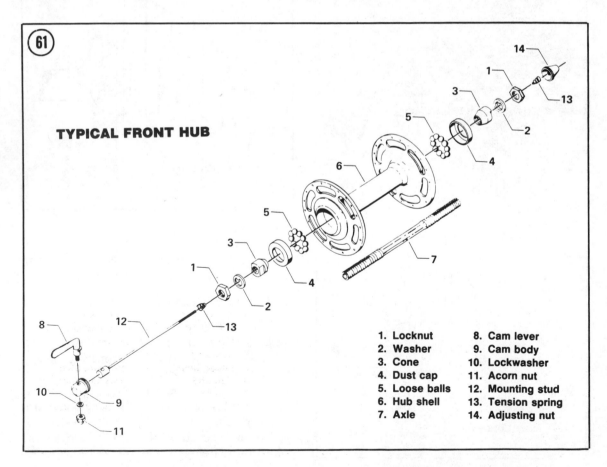

TYPICAL FRONT HUB

1. Locknut	8. Cam lever
2. Washer	9. Cam body
3. Cone	10. Lockwasher
4. Dust cap	11. Acorn nut
5. Loose balls	12. Mounting stud
6. Hub shell	13. Tension spring
7. Axle	14. Adjusting nut

b. Withdraw the mounting stud and other tension springs from the axle.

c. Fit all quick-release assembly parts together so that they will not get misplaced.

3. On derailleur-equipped bicycles, remove the freewheel cluster from the rear hub as described in this chapter.

4. Hold one cone with a cone wrench. Tighten the locknut against it with another wrench. If your hub does not have locknuts, tighten one of the axle mounting nuts against the cone.

5. Lay the wheel down so that the end of the axle tightened in Step 4 rests on a clean cloth.

6. Hold the locknut on the lower end of the axle with a wrench.

7. Loosen and remove the locknut (if any) and the cone from the upper end.

8. Slide the axle out of the hub assembly.

9A. On hubs with caged bearings, remove the bearings from the hub.

9B. On hubs with loose bearings, perform the following:

a. Pry out the upper dust cap with a wide-blade screwdriver.

b. Remove the balls. Take note of how many there are so that the same number can be installed.

c. Turn the hub over and remove the balls. Take note of how many there are so that the same number can be installed.

10. Leave the cone and locknut on the axle unless one of these parts is damaged. Before removing the damaged parts, measure the distance from the end of the axle to the top of the cone (**Figure 63**) so that the cone can be reinstalled in the proper position.

Inspection

1. Clean all parts thoroughly in solvent and dry with compressed air.

2. Inspect the cone and the hub shell bearing surfaces for pitting and excessive wear. Some

6

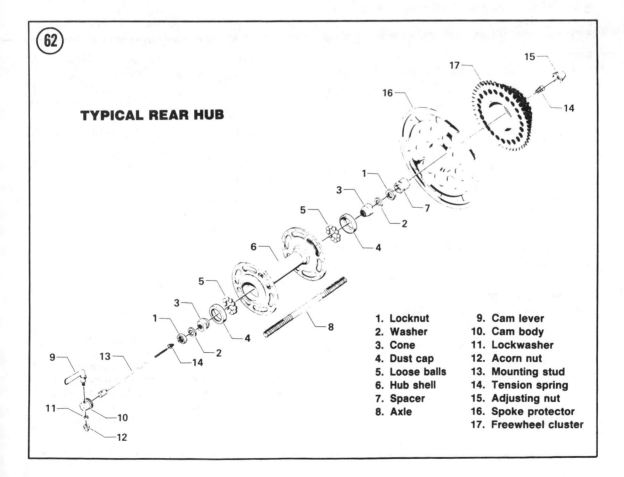

62

TYPICAL REAR HUB

1. Locknut	9. Cam lever
2. Washer	10. Cam body
3. Cone	11. Lockwasher
4. Dust cap	12. Acorn nut
5. Loose balls	13. Mounting stud
6. Hub shell	14. Tension spring
7. Spacer	15. Adjusting nut
8. Axle	16. Spoke protector
	17. Freewheel cluster

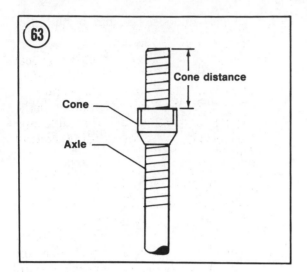

hubs have replaceable ball cups which provide the inner bearing surface. If these are worn, take the hub to your dealer to have new ball cups installed.

3. Inspect the ball bearings for pitting and wear. Replace as a complete set of balls if any are defective.

4. Check the dust caps (if any) for bends or nicks.

5. Check axle for bends or damaged threads.

6. Check the cone and locknut threads for damage.

Assembly

1. Install the cone to the position measured in *Disassembly* Step 10. Hold the cone in this position and tighten locknut against it.

2. Lubricate the hub bearing surfaces and ball bearings liberally with Lubriplate.

3A. On hubs with caged bearings, perform the following:

   a. Slide one bearing set on the axle so balls face away from cone.

   b. Slide the hub onto the axle.

   c. Install other bearing set over axle.

3B. On hubs with loose balls, perform the following:

   a. Install the dust cap on the axle.

   b. Slide the axle into the hub.

   c. Install the correct number of loose balls into hub.

   d. Install the dust cap into position and lightly tap it into the hub with a

hammer. Work around in a circle until the cap is squarely seated.

   e. Hold onto the axle so it will not slip out and turn the hub over.

   f. Install the corect number of loose balls in the other end of the hub.

   g. Install the other dust cap into position and lightly tap it into the hub with a hammer. Work around in a circle until the cap is squarely seated.

4. Install the remaining cone and locknut (if so equipped).

5. Tighten the cone hand-tight, then back off 1/8 turn.

6. Tighten the locknut against the cone hand-tight.

7. If so equipped, install the quick-release parts into the hub.

8. On derailleur-equipped bicycles, install freewheel cluster as described in this chapter.

POWER TRAIN TROUBLESHOOTING

1. *Grinding, rubbing or squeaking noises only while pedaling*—Trouble is worn, dirty or bent parts in the power train. Perform the following:

   a. Mount the bicycle in a repair stand.

   b. Slowly turn the pedals and check that the cranks do not rub on the kickstand or chain guard.

   c. Make sure that the chain does not rub the chain guard.

d. If nothing is obviously rubbing, remove the chain and turn the front sprocket. Any unusual noises are probably caused by internal bottom bracket damage.

e. Inspect the crankset as described in this chapter.

f. Check the pedals to be sure they spin smoothly and quietly. Lubricate or replace the pedals as described in this chapter.

2. *Same noises as in Step 1 whether pedaling or not*—Indicates worn or dry hubs or tire rubbing on frame or fenders. See Chapter Four for wheel alignment.

3. *Chain slips off or skips*—Perform the following:

a. First check chain tension as described in this chapter.

b. If trouble persists, check chainwheel and rear sprocket(s) for bent or missing teeth. Also check for a warped chainwheel. Bent teeth may be realigned by bending back with a crescent wrench. Work carefully so that the tooth does not break off and the sprocket is not warped.

c. Also check for a worn chain as described in this chapter.

4. *Chain won't move properly among chainwheels or chain rubs on front derailleur*—Perform the following:

a. Check adjustment of front derailleur as described in Chapter Three.

b. Check the position of derailleur on seat tube; refer to *Front Derailleur Removal/Installation* in this chapter.

c. Check for bent front derailleur parts, broken or binding control cable and excessively loose or binding control lever.

5. *Chain won't move properly among rear sprockets*—Perform the following:

a. Check adjustment of rear derailleur as described in Chapter Three.

b. Check for bent rear derailleur parts, broken or binding control cable and excessively loose or binding control lever.

6. *Pedal too loose, too tight, bent or broken*—Lubricate or replace the pedal as described in this chapter.

7. *Crank loose*—If cotterless or cottered cranks are loose, tighten *immediately* as described in this chapter or the crankset axle and cranks can be permanently damaged.

8. *Control lever too loose or difficult to move*—Ajust control lever tension by turning the wing nut or screw holding the lever assembly together (**Figure 64**). Disassemble and clean if necessary as described in this chapter.

6

Table 1 PEDAL IDENTIFICATION MARKS

Country of manufacture	Marking on right-hand pedal	Marking on left-hand pedal
England	R	L
France	D	G
Italy	D	S
Japan	R	L

CHAPTER SEVEN

SINGLE AND MULTI-SPEED POWER TRAINS

The power train on today's bicycles consists of a pedal-driven sprocket or sprockets linked to a rear wheel sprocket or sprockets via a chain.

Single-speed bicycles and multi-speed hub bicycles are very similar (**Figure 1**). Pedals attached to cranks drive a single front sprocket. The sprocket and crank assembly turn on an axle in the bottom bracket. The chain connects the front sprocket to a single rear sprocket. This sprocket is mounted on the rear wheel hub which provides a 1:1 (direct) drive ratio on single-speed bicycles or several different drive ratios on multi-speed hubs. The multi-speed hub is a complex arrangement of internal gears usually selected by moving a handlebar-mounted gear change lever (**Figure 2**).

Service to pedals, cranks and the bottom bracket is described in Chapter Six as these parts are similar to those used on derailleur equipped bicycles.

CHAIN

Inspection

The chain is one of the most severely stressed parts of the bicycle, yet is often neglected. Inspect the chain carefully whenever it is removed for cleaning as described in Chapter Three. It should also be inspected whenever it slips off or skips on the chainwheel.

To inspect the chain, remove it and clean thoroughly in solvent. Check that each link is flexible without binding, yet not too loose. Wrap the chain around the chainwheel (front sprocket) as shown in **Figure 3**. Pull the chain at the point indicated. If it can be pulled away from the chainwheel, it has stretched and must be replaced.

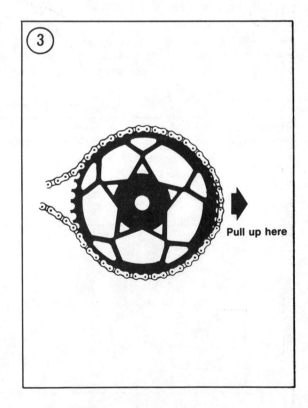

Pull up here

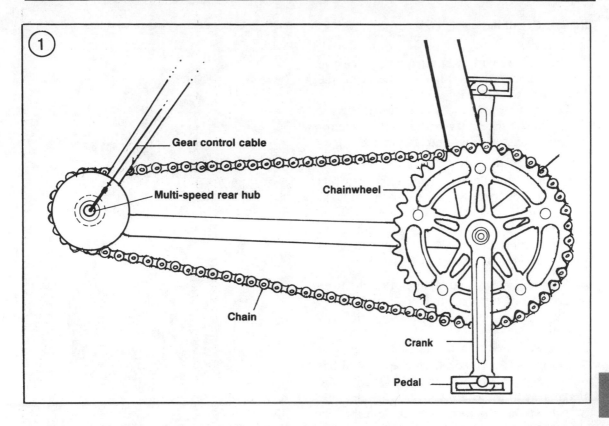

Gear control cable

Multi-speed rear hub

Chainwheel

Chain

Crank

Pedal

7

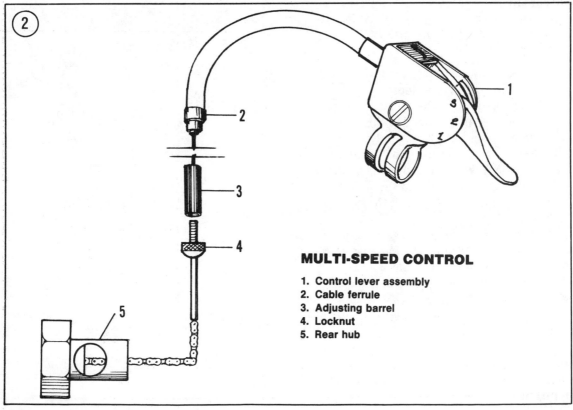

MULTI-SPEED CONTROL

1. Control lever assembly
2. Cable ferrule
3. Adjusting barrel
4. Locknut
5. Rear hub

Removal/Installation

1. On models with a coaster brake, remove the bolt and nut (A, **Figure 4**) securing the brake arm to the chain stay.
2. Loosen rear axle mounting nuts (B, **Figure 4**) and push wheel forward to slacken chain.
3. Find master link and disconnect it as follows:

  a. On some chains, a U-shaped plate fits between rollers; pry it to the side to remove it as shown in **Figure 5**.
  b. On other chains, a wide link plate identifies the master link; pry it off to remove it as shown in **Figure 6**.

4. Remove, clean and inspect the chain as described in Chapter Three.
5. Fit chain over the front and the rear sprockets.
6. Reconnect the master link.
7. On models with coaster brakes, install but do not tighten the bolt and nut securing the brake arm to the chain stay.
8. Adjust the chain tension as described in this chapter.

Repair

The chain must be repaired when a link becomes too tight or too loose.

If a link is too tight due to bent side plates, replace the link as described in this chapter. If the side plates are not bent, apply penetrating oil liberally to the link and flex it several times. If the link is still too tight, replace it.

To replace a link perform the following:
1. Insert the defective link in the chain rivet remover (**Figure 7**).
2. Screw the driving point against one of the rivets and drive it out. *Do not* drive it all the way out of the rear side plate.
3. Repeat Step 2 for the rivet on the other end of the defective link.
4. Insert the chain end in tool with the rivet *toward* the driving point.
5. Insert the new link in the tool and drive the rivet in.
6. Join the ends of the chain after it is reinstalled on the bicycle.

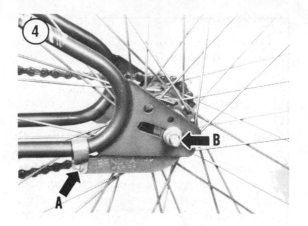

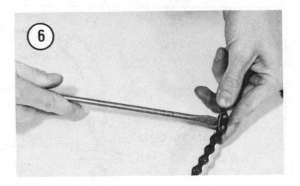

Tension Adjustment

Proper chain tension is important. If the tension is too loose, the chain may skip while pedaling, particularly in high gear where pedal effort is highest. If the tension is too high, pedaling effort and chain wear increase. Use as little chain tension as possible.

On single-speed or multi-speed hub bicycles, the chain free play should be 1/2 in. (13 mm) when pushed up midway between the sprockets on the lower chain run. See **Figure 8**. This free play should be measured while holding tension on pedals to keep the top portion of the chain run taut.

If adjustment is necessary, perform the following:

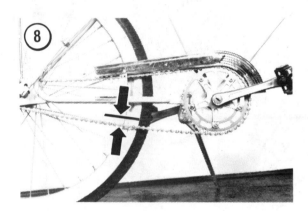

1. On models with a coaster brake, remove the bolt and nut (A, **Figure 4**) securing the brake arm to the chain stay.
2. Loosen rear axle mounting nuts (B, **Figure 4**) and move the wheel in either direction in the frame slots.
3. When the chain slack is less than 1/2 in. (13 mm), align the wheel rim within the chain stays and tighten the axle mounting nuts.
4. Rotate the rear wheel to move the chain to another position and recheck the adjustment; chains rarely wear or stretch evenly and, as a result, the free play will not remain constant over the entire chain. If the chain cannot be adjusted within these limits, it is excessively worn and stretched and should be replaced.
5. On models with coaster brakes, install and tighten the bolt and nut securing the brake arm to the chain stay.

REAR SPROCKET

Removal/Inspection/Installation

The rear sprocket can be attached to the rear hub by 2 different methods. The rear sprockets on some single-speed hubs are threaded onto the drive screw and secured with a lockring (**Figure 9**). Other sprockets are splined or lugged and then secured with a snap ring (**Figure 10**).

7

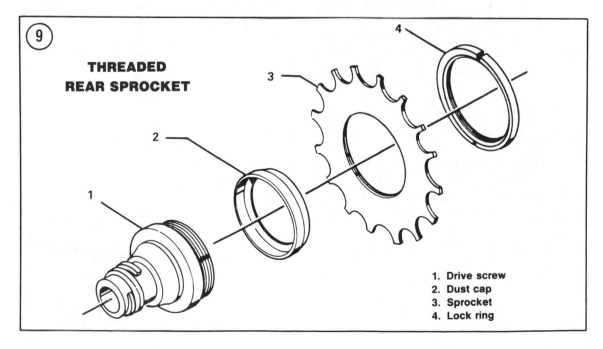

THREADED
REAR SPROCKET

1. Drive screw
2. Dust cap
3. Sprocket
4. Lock ring

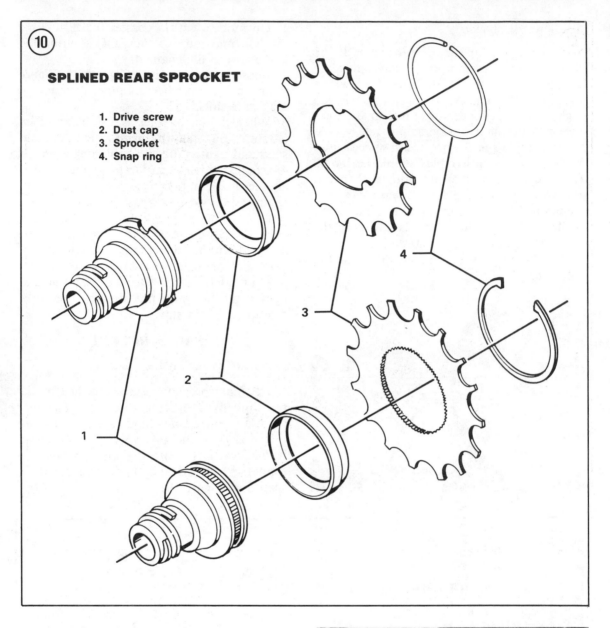

SPLINED REAR SPROCKET

1. Drive screw
2. Dust cap
3. Sprocket
4. Snap ring

Threaded sprocket

1. Remove the rear wheel as described in Chapter Four.
2. Clamp the hub in a vise with soft jaws, with the sprocket side facing up.
3. Hold the wheel rim with one hand and loosen the sprocket locknut *clockwise* with a hooked spanner wrench (**Figure 11**).
4. Remove the locknut from the hub.
5. Hold the wheel rim with one hand and loosen the sprocket *counterclockwise* with a sprocket tool (**Figure 12**).

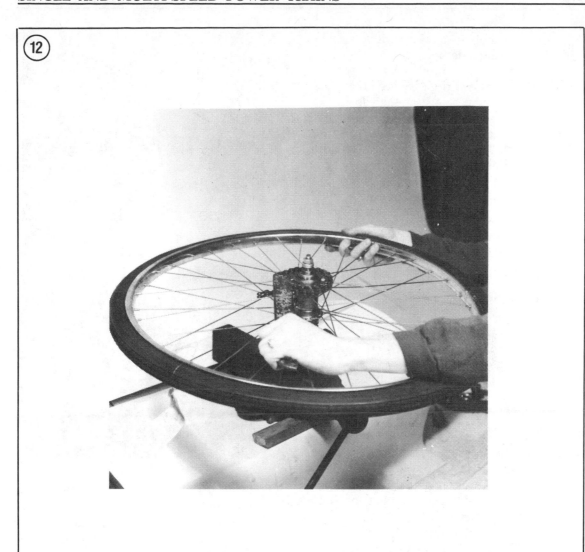

7

NOTE
The sprocket has an offset shoulder in the center. Note whether the shoulder is toward the inside or outside of the hub. Make a mark on the outside surface of the sprocket so it will be reinstalled correctly.

6. Remove the sprocket from the hub.
7. If so equipped, remove dust cap.
8. Inspect the sprocket and the drive screw for stripped or damaged threads. Replace if necessary.
9. Inspect the sprocket for worn or damaged teeth. Replace if necessary.
10. Inspect the dust cap for damage. Replace if necessary.

11. Install the dust cap.
12. Position the offset shoulder of the sprocket in the correct position. Refer to the mark made during removal.
13. Screw the sprocket onto the hub *clockwise* until finger-tight.
14. Hold the wheel rim with one hand. Tighten the sprocket *clockwise* with the sprocket tool.
15. Screw the locknut onto the drive screw *counterclockwise* and tighten with a hooked spanner wrench.

Lugged or splined sprocket

1. Remove the rear wheel as described in Chapter Four.

2. Clamp the hub in a vise with soft jaws, with the sprocket side up.

3A. For rounded snap rings, insert a narrow-bladed screwdriver between the drive screw and the snap ring near the gap in the ring. Pry the snap ring out of the groove and over the shoulder of the driver (**Figure 13**).

3B. For flat C-rings, hold one end of the C-ring stationary with your thumb. Using a screwdriver, force the other end to rotate around the groove until it snaps out.

> *NOTE*
> *The sprocket has an offset shoulder in the center. Note whether the shoulder is toward the inside or outside of the hub. Make a mark on the outside surface of the sprocket so it will be reinstalled correctly.*

> *NOTE*
> *The spacer washers may be between the snap ring and the sprocket or between the sprocket and the hub. This depends on the manufacturer. Carefully note the order of the parts removed so they may be reassembled in the same order later.*

4. Lift off the sprocket spacer washer(s), the sprocket and the dust cap.

5. Inspect the sprocket and the drive screw for stripped or damaged splines or lugs. Replace if necessary.

6. Inspect the sprocket teeth for wear or damage. Replace if necessary.

7. Inspect the dust cap for damage. Replace if necessary.

8. Install the dust cap, the sprocket and the spacer washer(s) in the order noted during disassembly.

9A. To install a rounded snap ring, perform the following:
   a. Position the opening between any 2 splines.
   b. Hold the snap ring with your thumb near the gap.
   c. Pry the snap ring over the drive screw shoulder with a screwdriver as shown in **Figure 14**.
   d. Lightly tap around the snap ring until it is firmly seated in the groove.

9B. To install a C-ring, perform the following:

a. Insert the tips of the C-ring in the groove on the drive screw.
b. Using a screwdriver, push the center of the C-ring toward the hub until the C-ring snaps into place.

CONTROL LEVER AND CABLE (MULTI-SPEED HUBS)

Control Lever Replacement

The control levers are usually simple, inexpensive devices. If the lever assembly becomes inoperative it should be replaced.

1. Disconnect the control cable as described in this chapter.

2. Loosen the clamp screw (**Figure 15**) securing the control lever to the handlebar and remove the lever assembly.

3. Install a new lever and tighten the clamp screw.

4. Reconnect the control cable as described in this chapter.

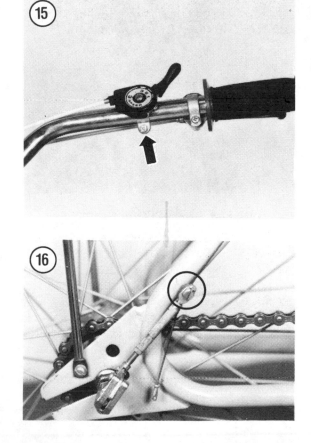

Control Cable Replacement

The control cable may be attached to the shift mechanism in a couple of different ways. Follow the correct steps for your specific model.

1A. If so equipped, loosen the screw (**Figure 16**) and nut securing the cable to the adjusting barrel.

1B. If so equipped, loosen the knurled locknut on the adjusting sleeve at the hub end of cable (**Figure 17**).

2. Unscrew the adjusting sleeve until the cable is free.

3. Disconnect the cable housing from the cable clips on the frame (**Figure 18**).

4. Disconnect the cable ferrule from the control lever body as follows:

    a. On some ferrules, pull upward until the threads engage with the control lever body threads, then unscrew the ferrule.

    b. On other ferrules, push the ferrule into the slot until it disengages from the lever (**Figure 19**).

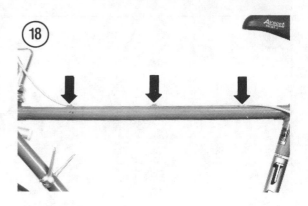

5. Pull the lever down past the lowest gear position.

6. Push the cable inward toward the control lever body to slacken the cable and disconnect the leaded end.

7. Pull the leaded end out between the pawl and the ratchet (**Figure 20**).

8. Pull the cable out through the ferrule hole.

9. Take the old cable and housing to a bicycle dealer. Purchase a new cable and housing of the same length and with the same shape cable ends.

10. Insert the proper end of cable through the ferrule hole in the control lever body. Run the cable between the pawl and the ratchet (**Figure 20**).

11. Hook the leaded end into the notch in the lever.

12. Screw the ferrule into the control lever body until it turns freely or insert in slot until it locks, depending on design.

13. Secure the cable housing in the cable clips on the frame. Hold tension on the hub end of cable and move the control lever to the highest gear.

14A. Reconnect the adjusting sleeve to the indicator rod on hub.

14A. Install the cable and tighten the screw (**Figure 16**) and nut securing the cable to the adjusting barrel.

15. Adjust the cable as described in Chapter Three.

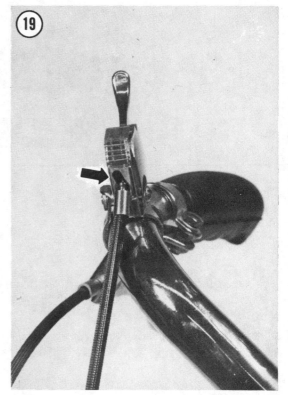

COASTER BRAKE HUBS

Coaster brake hubs are more complex than the hubs used on derailleur equipped bicycles. Due to their complexity it is suggested that you take either the entire bicycle or the rear

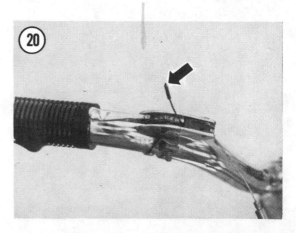

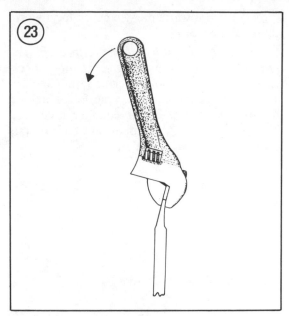

wheel assembly to a reputable bicycle dealer and let them work on the hub. Some special tools and a lot of experience are required to overhaul the hub. In many cases the hub can be replaced in the wheel or the entire wheel can be replaced.

The price of a complete hub (**Figure 21**) is relatively low compared to the cost of rebuilding an old hub and brake assembly.

MULTI-SPEED HUBS

There is a large range of multi-speed hubs in use. All are very complex and contain large numbers of very small parts. Due to their complexity it is suggested that you take either the entire bicycle or the rear wheel assembly to a reputable bicycle dealer and let them work on the hub. Some special tools and a lot of experience are required to overhaul the hub. In many cases the hub can be replaced in the wheel or the entire wheel can be replaced. The price of a complete hub (**Figure 22**) is relatively low compared to the cost of rebuilding an old hub.

TROUBLESHOOTING

1. *Grinding, rubbing or squeaking noises only while pedaling*—Trouble is worn, dirty or bent parts in the power train.

Mount the bicycle in a repair stand. Slowly turn the pedals and check that the cranks do not rub on the kickstand or chain guard. If nothing is obviously rubbing, remove the chain and turn the front sprocket. Any unusual noises are probably caused by internal bottom bracket damage. Check the pedals to make sure that they spin smoothly and quietly.

2. *Same noises as in Step 1 whether pedaling or not*—Indicates worn or dry hubs or tire rubbing on frame or fender. See Chapter Four for wheel alignment.

3. *Coaster brake doesn't stop or squeals excessively*—Lubricate coaster brake as described in Chapter Three. If trouble persists, have the hub overhauled or replaced as described in this chapter.

4. *Chain slips off or skips*—Check chain tension as described in this chapter. If trouble persists, check chainwheel and rear sprocket(s) for bent or missing teeth. Also check for a warped chainwheel. Bent teeth may be realigned by bending back with a crescent wrench (**Figure 23**). Work carefully so that the tooth does not break off and the

sprocket is not warped. Also check for a worn chain (**Figure 3**).

5. *Multi-speed hub gears slip, change unexpectedly or won't change at all*—Check cable adjustment as described in Chapter Three. Check the control cable for breaks or binding. Check the gear changer lever for binding. If the trouble appears to be internal, take the job to your dealer.

6. *Pedal too loose, too tight, bent or broken*—Adjust or replace pedal as described in Chapter Six.

7. *Crank loose*—If cotterless or cottered cranks are loose, tighten *immediately* or the crankset axle and cranks can be permanently damaged. Follow the procedures in Chapter Six.

CHAPTER EIGHT

FORK ASSEMBLY

The fork assembly consists of the handlebar, stem headset and fork (**Figure 1**). The front wheel attaches to the slotted ends of the fork blades, which bend forward slightly. This bend provides caster which adds stability to the bicycle. The amount of bend differs among the different types of bicycles.

The headset consists of a number of parts that hold the upper portion of the fork to the frame head tube. The headset bearings permit the fork to turn smoothly. The stem fits into the top of the fork and is held in place with an expander bolt. A bolt clamps the handlebar to the stem and permits the bars to be adjusted to any position.

The fork is normally made of the same materials as the frame. Fork members are joined by welding or brazing, similar to frame members.

HANDLEBAR

Removal/Installation

1A. On a taped handlebar, pull out both end plugs and unwrap the tape.

1B. On a non-taped handlebar, remove one of the hand grips (A, **Figure 2**).

①

FORK ASSEMBLY
1. Stem
2. Handlebar
3. Headset
4. Fork

8

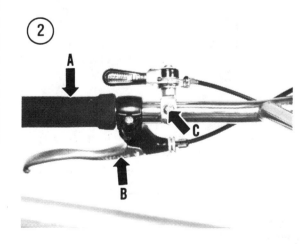
②

2. On models so equipped, loosen or remove the screws and nuts securing the caliper brake hand levers (B, **Figure 2**) and gear shifters (C, **Figure 2**). Remove both caliper brake lever assemblies and gear shifters.

3A. On models with an integral handlebar/stem assembly, perform the following:

    a. Loosen the stem binder bolt (**Figure 3**).

    b. Using a plastic or rubber mallet, tap on the bolt lightly to force the taper plug out of the bottom of the stem.

    c. Withdraw the assembly from the steering head.

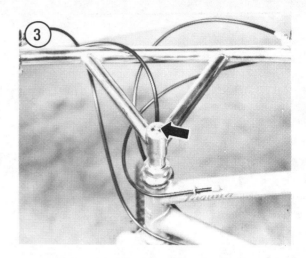

NOTE
The type of binder bolt and its location will vary.

3B. On all other models, perform the following:

    a. Loosen binder bolt in the stem. Refer to **Figure 4** or **Figure 5**.

    b. Carefully withdraw the handlebar through the hole in the stem. On non-taped handlebars, be careful to not scratch the plating on the handlebar.

    c. Completely remove the handlebar.

4. Install by reversing these removal steps; note the following.

5. To maintain a good grip on the handlebar and to prevent it from slipping down, clean the knurled section of the handlebar with a wire brush. It should be kept rough so it will be held securely by the holders. The holding portion of the stem should also be kept clean and free of any metal gouged loose by handlebar slippage.

6. On a taped handlebar, retape the handlebar as described in this chapter.

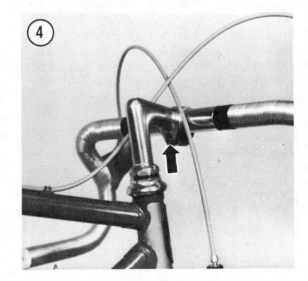

Retaping

Replacement handlebar tape is available in adhesive backed cloth or plastic. Plastic tape without adhesive backing is also available. Choice is a matter of preference. All types stick well and provide a good, comfortable grip.

1. Remove each end plug and unwrap the old tape.

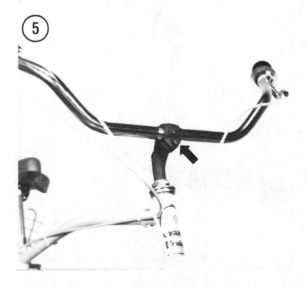

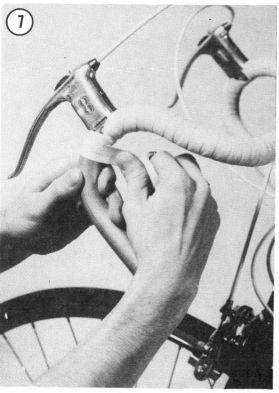

2. Clean off any old adhesive residue on the handlebar surface with a solvent that does not leave an oily residue.

3. Start wrapping the new tape about 2 in. (50 mm) from the middle of the bar (**Figure 6**). If using non-adhesive tape, stick the end down with a piece of cellophane tape. Wrap a few turns over the end to cover the tape.

4. Continue working downward toward the brake lever. Overlap about 1/3 of the tape width onto the previously wrapped tape (**Figure 7**). Do not leave any gaps where the metal will show through.

5. When you reach the end of the bar, push 2-3 in. (50-75 mm) of tape inside the bar (**Figure 8**).

NOTE
Plugs are available in different outside diameters to fit different size handlebars. Be sure you buy the right size.

6. Plug the end with a plastic bar plug (**Figure 9**). This secures the tape and gives a finished look to the job.

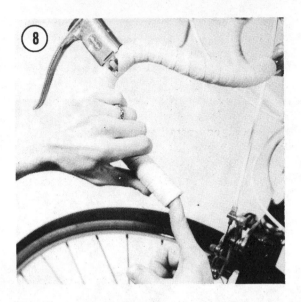

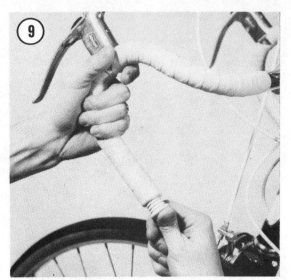

STEM

The stem fits into the top section of the fork. The expander bolt pulls up on a tapered plug in the bottom of the stem (**Figure 10**). The tapered plug expands in the top section of the fork and holds the stem in place.

Due to the stress placed on the handlebar and stem in BMX racing, various heavy-duty stems are available. Most have a wider surface (**Figure 11**) to get a better bite on the handlebar and help prevent it from slipping.

Removal/Installation

1A. On models with an integral handlebar/stem assembly, perform the following:
  a. Loosen the stem binder bolt (**Figure 3**).
  b. Using a plastic or rubber mallet, tap on the bolt lightly to force the taper plug out of the bottom of the stem.
  c. Withdraw the assembly from the steering head.
1B. On models with a separate handlebar and stem, perform the following:
  a. Remove the handlebar as described in this chapter if the stem is going to be replaced.
  b. Loosen the expander bolt (**Figure 12**) on the stem 2 or 3 turns. It is not necessary to remove it.

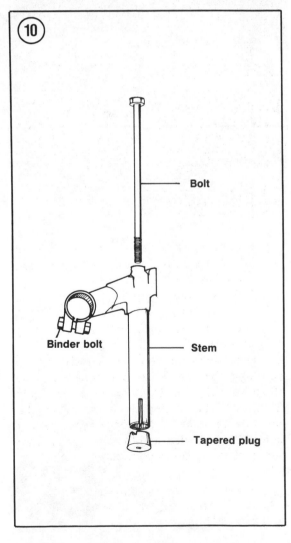

Bolt

Binder bolt

Stem

Tapered plug

3A. On models with an integral handlebar/stem assembly, install the assembly into the steering head.

3B. On all other models, install the stem into the steering head.

4. While pulling up on the expander bolt to seat the taper plug, tighten the bolt by hand.

5. If removed, install the handlebar.

6. Hold the front wheel straight ahead. Align the handlebars with the wheel. Tighten the expander bolt securely to hold the stem in place.

FORK AND HEADSET

The headset consists of individual components within the head tube. These components secure the fork to the head tube of the frame and permit it to turn. **Figures 13-15** show several typical headsets. The main difference is in the type of ball bearings used. Some have assembled (caged) ball bearings; others have loose ball bearings.

Suntour offers a headset lock-up unit (**Figure 16**) that helps to keep the headset from working loose during hard riding. The small Allen bolts (with nylon bushings) tighten against the fork threads and hold the locknut in place.

8

c. Using a plastic or rubber mallet, tap the bolt head lightly to force the taper plug out of the bottom of the stem.

d. Pull the stem up and out. If necessary, hold the front wheel stationary and twist the stem back and forth while pulling upward.

2. If the stem is going to be replaced, take the stem and the handlebar to a bicycle dealer. Make sure the inside diameter of the new stem handlebar clamp is the same as the outside diameter of the handlebar. If the handlebar is smaller than the clamp, purchase a shim to make up the difference.

CAUTION
*For stability, insert a **minimum** of 2 1/2 in. (74 mm) of the stem down in the head tube.*

Disassembly

1. Remove the handlebar and stem (A, **Figure 17**) as described in this chapter.

2. Remove the front wheel as described in this chapter.

3. Remove the brake caliper assembly from the fork as described in Chapter Five.

4. Remove the locknut (B, **Figure 17**) and the keyed washer (C, **Figure 17**) from the headset.

5. On models so equipped, remove the cable hanger for center-pull brakes.

6. Lay the bicycle on its side with a clean cloth under the head tube.

7. Remove the threaded adjustable race (D, **Figure 17**).

8. Hold the fork tightly against the head tube so that the bottom bearings cannot fall out.

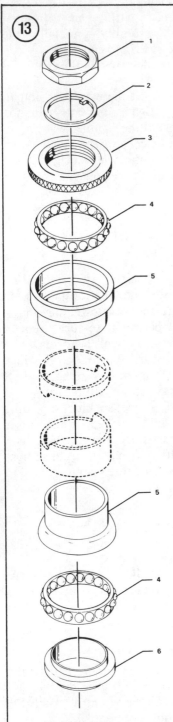

⑬

1. Locknut
2. Washer
3. Adjustable race
4. Bearing
5. Bearing race
6. Fork crown race

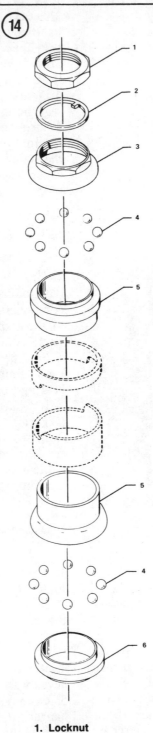

⑭

1. Locknut
2. Washer
3. Adjustable race
4. Bearing
5. Bearing race
6. Fork crown race

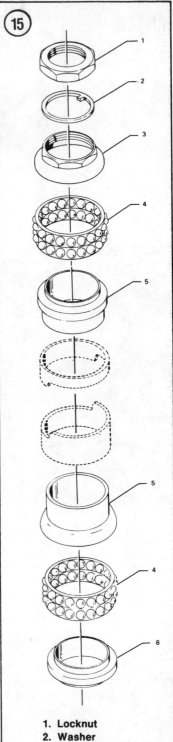

⑮

1. Locknut
2. Washer
3. Adjustable race
4. Bearing
5. Bearing race
6. Fork crown race

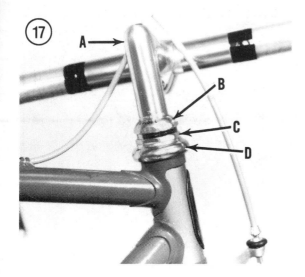

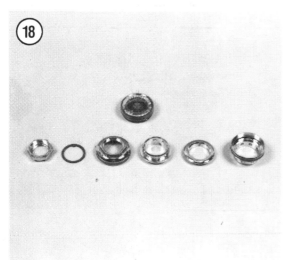

9. Place a large pan under the upper portion of the head tube to catch any loose ball bearings if they fall out.

10A. Remove the upper ball bearings while still holding the fork against the head tube. If equipped with loose ball bearings, count them and write the number down so that the same number can be reinstalled.

10B. If equipped with assembled (caged) ball bearings, remove the assembly from the top of the head tube.

11. Move the large pan under the lower portion of the head tube to catch any loose ball bearings if they fall out.

12. Slowly remove the fork from the head tube.

13A. The bottom ball bearings will fall out if they are loose. Count them and write the number down so that the same number can be reinstalled.

13B. If equipped with assembled (or caged) ball bearings, slide the assembly off the fork.

NOTE
Keep the upper bearings and the lower bearings separate from each other as the size and quantity may vary.

Inspection

1. Clean the bearing races in the steering head, the steering stem races and the bearings with solvent and thoroughly dry.

2. Check the welds or brazing arond the steering head for cracks and fractures. These may be indicated by cracks in the paint or a gap where 2 metal pieces join.

3. Check the fork blades for bends, cracks or dents.

4. Check the bearings for pitting, scratches or discoloration indicating wear. Replace them in sets if necessary; take old bearings to a bicycle dealer to make sure you get exact replacements (**Figure 18**).

5. Check the upper and lower headset bearing races, fork crown race and top adjustable race for pitting, scratches or discoloration indicating wear. If any of these conditions exist, replace the bearing races as described in this chapter.

8

Bearing Race Replacement

The headset and fork crown bearing races are pressed into place. Because they are easily bent, do not remove them unless they are worn and require replacement.

Headset bearing race removal/installation

> *NOTE*
> *The upper and lower bearing races are usually of a different size. Be sure that you install them at the proper ends of the head tube.*

Take old races (**Figure 18**) to a bicycle dealer to make sure you get an exact replacement.

1. To remove the headset race, insert a hardwood stick into the head tube (**Figure 19**) and carefully tap the race out from the inside.
2. After it is started, tap around the race so that neither the race nor the head tube are damaged.
3. Repeat for the other bearing race.
4. To install a race, fit it into the end of the head tube. Make sure that the race is squarely seated in the headset race bore before tapping it into place.
5. Tap it slowly and squarely in with a block of wood (**Figure 20**).
6. Tap the bearing race in until it is flush with the steering head surface.

Fork crown race removal/installation

1. To remove the fork crown race from the fork, try twisting and pulling it by hand. If it is stuck carefully pry it up with a screwdriver, working around in a circle, prying a little at a time.
2. To install the fork crown race, slide it over the fork tube with the bearing surface pointing up. Tap the race down with a piece of hardwood; work around in a circle so that the race will not be bent (**Figure 21**). Make sure it is seated squarely and is all the way down.

Assembly

1. Make sure the headset races and the fork crown race are correctly installed and seated.

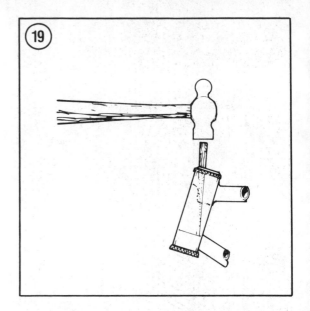

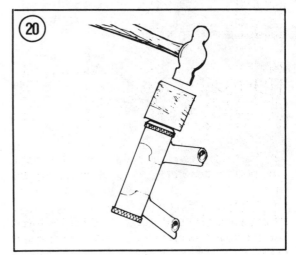

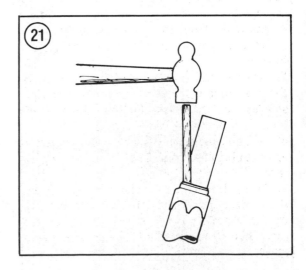

2. Turn the bicycle upside down. Lubricate the bottom headset race with Lubriplate light grease.

3. Apply Lubriplate to the bearings. Install the correct size and number of ball bearings or the caged bearing in the bottom headset race. The grease will hold loose bearings in place.

4. Insert the front fork tube into the headset. Be careful not to accidentally dislodge the bearings.

5. Have an assistant hold the fork tight aginst the head tube while you turn the bicycle right side up. Do not let the fork slip down or the loose ball bearings may fall out.

6. Still holding the fork against the head tube, apply Lubriplate light grease to upper headset race.

7. Apply Lubriplate to the bearings. Install the correct size and number of ball bearings or the caged bearing in the upper headset race. The grease will hold loose bearings in place.

8. Screw the adjustable race onto the headset.

9. Tighten the adjustable race hand-tight, then back off 1/4 turn.

10. Install the front wheel as described in this chapter.

11. Install the flat keyed washer and the locknut.

12. Tighten the locknut securely.

13. Adjust the headset as described in this chapter.

14. If removed, install the front brake caliper.

15. Install the handlebar and the stem as described in this chapter.

Headset Adjustment

If the fork turns stiffly or has excess play, it may require adjustment.

1. Loosen the locknut (B, **Figure 17**).

2. Loosen the adjustable race (D, **Figure 17**), tighten it hand-tight, then back off (counterclockwise) 1/4 turn. Tighten the locknut.

3. Turn the wheel back and forth. If it feels stiff, loosen the locknut and loosen the adjustable race another 1/4 turn. Tighten the locknut. If wheel still feels stiff, the headset requires overhaul. Disassemble, inspect and reassemble as described in this chapter.

4. To check the fork for excessive play, perform the following:

    a. Lift the front wheel clear of the ground, then set it down; look for vertical play (**Figure 22**).

    b. Now hold the handlebar stem with one hand and a fork blade with the other. Try to wiggle the assembly from side to side, looking for horizontal play (**Figure 23**).

    c. If there is any vertical or horizontal play, loosen the locknut and tighten the adjustable race 1/4 turn. Tighten the locknut and recheck play. If still present, disassemble, inspect and reassemble as described in this chapter.

Repairing Bends

Refer to **Figure 24** for places to check for bends, distortion and damage.

Repairing damaged forks is practically impossible. It is not recommended except in

8

an emergency while touring. Purchase a new fork rather than risk poor handling, excessive tire wear or even injury if a fork should break.

A bent fork may be repaired in an emergency by slipping a section of pipe over the bent area. With brute force, bend the fork back as close as possible to its original shape. This method nearly always results in a nick in the metal at the top of the pipe or an undetectable crack. The fork can easily break at this point.

WARNING
Ride slowly. The fork can easily crack and break at this point and cause serious injury. Replace the fork as soon as possible.

TROUBLESHOOTING

1. *Loose handlebars*—Usually caused by loose binder bolt. Adjust the handlebar to the most comfortable position and tighten binder bolt.

2. *Loose stem*—Caused by loose expander bolt. Hold the front wheel straight ahead, align the handlebar with wheel and tighten the expander bolt.

3. *Steering stiff or noisy*—The headset requires either adjustment, lubrication or repair. See appropriate procedures in this chapter. Lubrication requires disassembly and assembly.

4. *Steering very loose with vertical and/or horizontal play*—The headset requires either adjustment or repair. See appropriate procedures in this chapter.

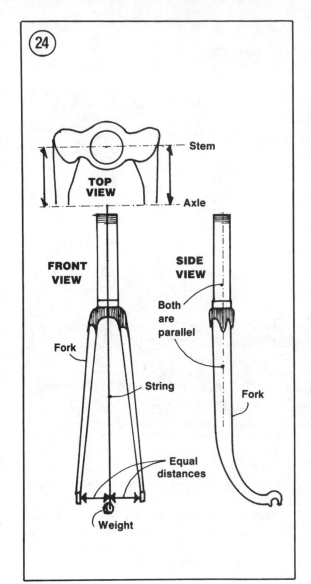

CHAPTER NINE

FRAME

The frame consists of 3 main tubes forming a triangle and 2 pairs of smaller tubes supporting the rear wheel. These tubular steel members are joined by welding or brazing at the head, crank hub, seat mast, tube and rear axle (**Figure 1**).

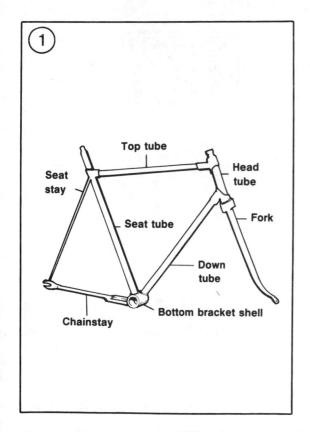

The frame of the bicycle is the heart of the entire machine. Not only does it serve as a mounting point for all the other components, it also determines to a great extent what kind of ride you will get. If the frame is too stiff, it will transmit every bump in the road and handle poorly in curves. If the frame is too springy, it will whip and bend when you pedal and pull on the handlebars. The ride will be "rubbery" and the frame will absorb some of the energy which is meant to propel you forward.

A good frame maker strikes a balance between stiff and springy, creating a frame which is lively and responsive. Design, construction methods and materials are selected to produce a frame with the desired qualities.

In today's market of highly specialized frames you can order almost any particular design of frame that best suits your needs.

FRAME DESIGN

Frame design is a rather complex art which is beyond the scope of a repair manual. On custom frames, the dimensions and angles of every tube can be selected to suit the owner's body dimensions, preferences and the type of riding (racing, touring, etc.). For stock frames, the maker must compromise somewhat to make a frame which is useful for general riding.

METALS

Most bicycle frames use steel alloys for the tubing. An alloy is a mixture of metals which have qualities that no one metal alone has, e.g., low weight, high strength, high corrosion resistance, etc. Alloys with low carbon content and high tensile strength make thinner tubing possible.

Most manufacturers use steel-molybdenum alloy for bicycles. Molybdenum added to steel promotes structural uniformity and increases hardness and stress endurance.

Reynolds of England is the major manufacturer of manganese-molybdenum

REYNOLDS TUBING IDENTIFICATION

Only the top tube, seat tube and down tube are made with Reynolds 531 plain gauge tubing.

Only the top tube, seat tube and down tube are made with Reynolds 531 butted tubing.

All tubing in bicycle made with Reynolds 531 plain gauge tubing.

All tubing in bicycle made with Reynolds 531 butted tubing.

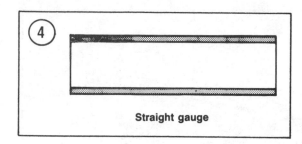

Straight gauge

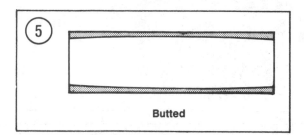

Butted

alloy steel bicycle tubing. This tubing is marketed as "Reynolds 531" in straight and double-butted design. Look for the "Reynolds 531" sticker (**Figure 2**) when purchasing a frame. Columbus tubing and Falk tubing are of comparable quality, but not as well known.

Decals identify Reynolds tubing and explain the extent and type of tubing used in the bicycle (**Figure 3**). If in doubt about the tubing used in your frame, ask your dealer.

TUBING DESIGN

Most bicycles use cold-drawn seamless tubing. This type tubing has the greatest strength for the least weight. Only very inexpensive bicycles use seamed (welded) tubing. Seamless tubing may be straight gauge or butted.

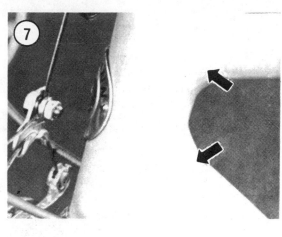

Straight Gauge Tubing

As the name implies, this tubing is uniformly thick throughout its length (**Figure 4**). The principle advantage of straight gauge tubing is its strength, but at the expense of lightness.

Butted Tubing

A bit more sophisticated, butted tubing combines lightest weight with the greatest strength. It is thickest at the ends where greatest stress occurs and tapers gradually to its thinnest point at the middle (**Figure 5**).

CONSTRUCTION

Two methods of joining frame members can be used. Some manufacturers join members by low-temperature brazing. Other manufacturers weld the members together. There is no general agreement as to which is best.

Low-temperature Brazing

Both brass and bronze will flow onto a properly cleaned, heated surface and give a very strong bond, although the base metal is not actually melted. Brazing can be likened to an adhesive. Lugs are necessary to give increased strength at the joints (**Figure 6**).

Welding

This is the process of joining pieces of metal by heating until the metals themselves melt and flow together. This gives the joint high tensile strength (**Figure 7**).

9

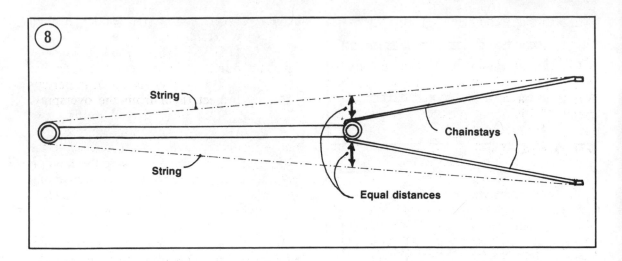

REPAIRS

Damage to a frame is almost inevitable. When it happens, the frame should be stripped of all components and replaced, especially if the bicycle is a high-priced, lightweight model.

When frame tubing is bent, regardless of how neatly a repair is made, the damaged area is a weak point susceptible to more extensive damage in the future.

Refer to **Figure 8** and **Figure 9** to check your frame to see if it is bent or out of alignment.

RECONDITIONING

Reconditioning is limited to stripping components, cleaning and preparation for repainting. Stripping the bike also allows you to perform maintenance and lubrication described in Chapter Three.

Component Removal

Remove the components by following a systematic procedure. Keep the many parts of each component together.

1. Remove accessories such as horns, lights and carriers.
2. Loosen the seat mast bolt. Remove the seat post with the seat attached.
3. Remove the brake calipers; disconnect the cables from calipers. Refer to Chapter Five.
4. On derailleur equipped bicycles, loosen the clamp holding the shift levers. Release the cables from the front and rear derailleurs.

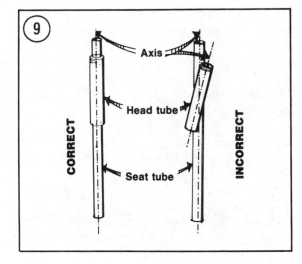

5A. On derailleur equipped bicycles, remove the front and rear derailleurs. Remove the rear wheel as described in Chapter Six.
5B. On multi-speed hub bicycles, disconnect the shifter cable from the hub. Remove the rear wheel as described in Chapter Seven.
6. Remove the chain.
7. Remove the cranks, front sprockets and chain guard as described in Chapter Six.
8. Remove the front wheel as described in Chapter Four.
9. Remove the handlebars and front fork assembly as described in Chapter Eight.
10. Remove all cable guides that are clamped to frame.
11. If so equipped, remove the fenders.
12. Assemble by reversing these removal steps.

Stripping and Painting

Remove all components from the frame. Thoroughly strip off all old paint. The best way is to have it sandblasted down to bare metal. If this is not possible, you can use a liquid paint remover and steel wool and a fine, hard wire brush. If the frame is an expensive one, have it inspected for hairline and internal cracks after stripping. Magnaflux is the most common and complete process.

If you do not strip the frame completely you must sand the old paint down to at least the original color or primer. All scratches or nicks should be feather-edged by sanding the damaged area and surrounding area until the entire area is smooth. Sand it until you can no longer feel the ridge of the scratch with your fingers. Final wet sanding should be done with No. 400 wet/dry sandpaper. Be sure to throughly wash off the frame to remove all old paint residue.

If there are any chrome plated areas (end of forks on some models), they must be masked off with masking tape and paper. Seal the entire area off as paint overspray will creep through almost any open area in the paper.

Stuff paper into the bottom bracket receptacle to prevent the threads from getting clogged with paint. Also carefully apply some grease to the threads; don't get any of the grease on the surrounding area that is to be painted.

If the bicycle has an ornate head tube medallion it should be covered so it will not get painted. Use a small artist's paint brush and apply several coats of liquid automobile wax to the medallion. Be careful not to get wax on the head tube as the paint will not stick where there is any wax.

It is recommended that the fork be left attached to the frame. That way the color will be consistant from the frame to the fork. This is especially true if you are going to use a 2-step color with a base color (usually silver or gold) and final transparent color. If painted separately, one of the components is going to have a different color valuc.

Tie the frame up to the rafters in the garage or support it with rope on the shelf of a step ladder. If you use a step ladder it then becomes a portable unit.

Prepare the area where you are going to paint the frame. If you are going to spray the frame in your garage, cover up all important items to protect them from the overspray. Use old blankets, drop cloths and newspapers. Thoroughly vacuum the floor and surrounding area. Let the dust settle for about 1/2 hour, then wet down the floor to help settle any remaining dust. After doing this, move around carefully in the area and do not move any items that may stir up additional dust.

If you are going to spray the frame outside, do it in the morning when the air tends to be still.

Prior to painting the frame, use a lintless cloth with some lacquer thinner and wipe down the entire frame. This will help remove any paint, skin oil from your hands or other foreign particles prior to painting.

Make sure that the primer is compatible with the type of paint you are going to use for the finish color. Spray on one or two coats of primer as smoothly as possible. Let it dry thoroughly and use a fine grade of wet/dry sandpaper (400-600 grit) to remove any flaws. Carefully wipe the surface clean with a lintless cloth and then spray a couple of coats of the final color. Use either lacquer or enamel base paint and follow the manufacturer's instructions.

NOTE
If you ride in wet areas or live near the ocean, you may want to consider a rust preventive formula paint. This may help to extend the life of the frame.

A shop specializing in painting will probably do the best job. However, you can do a surprisingly good job with a good grade of spray paint. Spend a few extra dollars and get a good grade of paint as it will make a difference in how well it looks and how long it will stand up. It's a good idea to shake the can and make sure the ball inside the can is loose when you purchase the can of paint. Shake the can as long as is stated on the can. Then immerse the can *upright* in a pot or bucket of *warm* water (not over 120° F).

9

WARNING
*Higher temperatures could cause the can to burst. **Do not** place the can in direct contact with any flame or heat source.*

Leave the can in the water for several minutes. When thoroughly warmed, shake the can again and spray the frame. Be sure to get into all the crevices where there may be rust problems. Several light mist coats are better than one heavy coat. Spray painting is best done in temperatures of 70-80° F (21-26° C); any temperature above or below this will give you problems.

After the final coat has dried completely, at least 48 hours, any overspray or orange peel may be removed with a *light application* of Dupont rubbing compound (red color) and finished with Dupont polishing compound (white color). Be careful not to rub too hard or you will go through the finish.

Remove the wax and unwanted paint from the headtube medallion with a stiff toothbrush. Remove any masking tape and paper from the forks.

Finish off with a couple coats of good wax prior to reassembling all the components.

It's a good idea to keep the frame touched up with fresh paint if any minor rust spots or scratches appear.

CHAPTER TEN

ASSEMBLING AND ADJUSTING
A BICYCLE

This chapter describes how to assemble a new bicycle. In addition, there are recommendations for adjusting the bicycle to fit your body dimensions and preferences.

ASSEMBLING A NEW BICYCLE

When you buy a fully assembled bicycle from a reputable bicycle dealer, you are assured of a properly assembled and carefully adjusted machine. Buying from a discount or department store is not the same. The bicycle is probably assembled by an unskilled stock clerk who does not have the experience or the proper tools required to do a good job. You are probably better off buying an unassembled bicycle and saving the assembly fee. Assemble the bicycle yourself with the manufacturer's instruction booklet and the guidelines in this chapter. Expect to spend about 2 hours to assemble the bicycle properly.

Derailleur Equipped

These include 5-, 10-, 15- and 18-speed derailleur bicycles with hand-operated caliper brakes.
1. Open the carton or unwrap it carefully and remove all the parts. Don't throw away any packing materials until the bicycle is completely assembled and all parts accounted for.
2. Find the instruction booklet and read it from cover to cover.
3. Untie or untape all parts that are fastened to the frame.
4. Remove all the protective wrapping from the frame.
5. Loosen the front axle nuts. If they are tight, hold one with a wrench while loosening the other with a second wrench.
6. Install the front wheel in the fork, center the wheel and tighten the mounting nuts or quick-release lever. Spin the wheel to make sure it is true.
7. Install the rear wheel in the frame, center the wheel and tighten the mounting nuts or quick-release lever. Spin the wheel to make sure it is true.
8. Install the kickstand as described by the manufacturer.

NOTE
By installing both wheels and the kickstand, the bike can be propped upright for the remaining assembly.

9. Insert the handlebar stem in the head tube a minimum of 2-3 in. (50-75 mm). This will be adjusted later to fit your body dimensions.

10

Tighten the stem bolt (**Figure 1**) just enough to keep the stem from slipping.

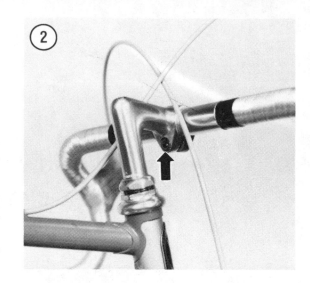

NOTE
Many manufacturers mount the handlebars in the stem, have the brake levers in place and have taped the bars. Steps 10-11 may be unnecessary.

10. Insert the handlebar in the stem and tighten the clamp bolt snugly (**Figure 2**). This will be adjusted more precisely later.

11. Mount the brake levers in place on the handlebar. Exact position will be adjusted later. Do not tape the bars yet, as lever position cannot be changed with the tape in place. Refer to Chapter Five, *Hand Lever Removal/Installation*, for more details.

12. Mount the saddle (A, **Figure 3**) on the post. Tighten the clamp bolt securely.

13. Insert the seat post into the frame. Tighten the clamp bolt (B, **Figure 3**) just enough to keep the post from slipping. This will be adjusted later.

14. Mount the rear brake caliper on the frame (**Figure 4**). Most manufacturers do this themselves. For more details on mounting the brakes, refer to Chapter Five.

15. Mount the front brake caliper on the fork (**Figure 5**). Refer to Chapter Five for more details on mounting the brakes.

16. Install the front and rear brake cables as described in Chapter Five.

17. Align the brake shoes and adjust the brakes as described in Chapter Three.

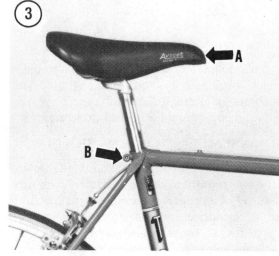

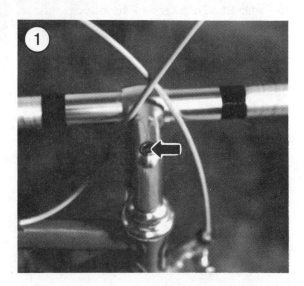

18. Install the pedals (**Figure 6**). Note that one has right-hand threads while the other has left-hand threads; they are not interchangeable. To tighten the pedals in the crank, turn the wrench toward the front of the bike while looking at the pedal.

19. Check the front derailleur position. The bottom of the chain guide should be about 3/16 in. (5 mm) above the teeth on the largest sprocket (**Figure 7**). The chain guide must also be parallel to the sprockets. Loosen the clamp screws if necessary to adjust derailleur position.

20. Mount the bicycle in a repair stand like that shown in Chapter Two or have an assistant hold the rear wheel off the ground.

21. Carefully adjust the front derailleur as described in Chapter Three.

22. Carefully adjust the rear derailleur as described in Chapter Three.

23. Inflate the tires to the recommended pressure listed in Chapter Three.

24. Adjust the saddle and handlebar position as described in this chapter.

25. Adjust brake lever position as described in this chapter. If the manufacturer has already mounted the levers and taped the bars, do not hesitate to remove the tape and reposition the levers as desired.

26. If necessary, tape handlebars as described in Chapter Eight.

Single- or Multi-speed

These include single-speed bicycles with a coaster brake and bicycles with multi-speed rear hubs with coaster or caliper handbrakes.

1. Open the carton or unwrap it carefully and remove all the parts. Don't throw away any packing materials until the bicycle is completely assembled and all parts accounted for.

2. Find the instruction booklet and read it from cover to cover.

3. Untie or untape all parts that are fastened to the frame.

4. Remove all the protective wrapping from the frame.

5. Loosen the front axle nuts. If they are tight, hold one with a wrench while loosening the other with a second wrench.

10

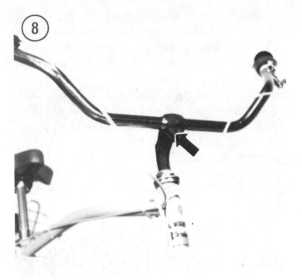

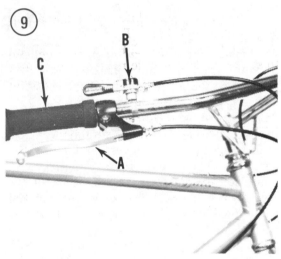

6. Install the front wheel in the fork, center the wheel and tighten the mounting nuts or quick-release lever. Spin the wheel to make sure it is true.

7. Install the rear wheel in the frame, center the wheel and tighten the mounting nuts or quick-release lever. Spin the wheel to make sure it is true.

8. Install the kickstand as described by the manufacturer.

9. Slide the handlebars through the stem and tighten the clamp bolt snugly (**Figure 8**).

10. If so equipped, mount the handbrake levers (A, **Figure 9**). The rear brake lever goes on the right-hand side and the front brake lever goes on the left-hand side.

11. Mount the rear brake caliper on the frame (**Figure 10**). Most manufacturers have already installed this item. For more details on mounting different types of brakes refer to Chapter Five.

12. Mount the front brake caliper on the fork (**Figure 11**). Refer to Chapter Five for more details on mounting the brakes.

13. Install the front and rear brake cables as described in Chapter Five.

14. Align the brake shoes and adjust the brakes as described in Chapter Three.

15. Install the pedals (**Figure 12**). Note that one has right-hand threads while the other has left-hand threads; they are not interchangeable. To tighten the pedals in the crank, turn the wrench toward the front of the bike while looking at the pedal.

16. Mount the saddle (A, **Figure 13**) on the post. Tighten the clamp bolt securely.

17. Insert the seat post into the frame. Tighten the clamp bolt (B, **Figure 13**) just enough to keep the post from slipping. This will be adjusted later.

18. On multi-speed bicycles, mount the gear shifter (B, **Figure 9**) on the handlebars or the frame as directed by the manufacturer.

19. Connect the gear shifter cable and adjust as described in Chapter Threet.

20. Install hand grips (C, **Figure 9**). If difficult to slide on, apply a little moist bar soap as a lubricant. When the soap dries, the grips will not slip.

ADJUSTING BICYCLE DIMENSIONS

Frame Height

Correct frame size is very important for both comfort and safety. If the frame is too big, it is difficult to get on and off. If the frame is too small, pedal efficiency is low.

Frame sizes generally range from 19 1/2-25 1/2 in. (49.5-64.7 mm). Size is determined by measuring the distance from the center of the crank hub to the top of the frame where the seat post is inserted (A, **Figure 14**).

Generally, you should be able to straddle the frame with your feet flat on the ground. There are several pet formulas to choose the correct frame. Most of these compute a frame size 6-9 in. (15.2-22.9 mm) less than the measurement from your crotch to the floor in stocking feet. For touring bikes, choose a slightly smaller frame.

Saddle Adjustment

Saddle position greatly affects comfort and efficiency. Most people tend to adjust the saddle too low. This makes it difficult to use your leg muscles most efficiently.

10

As with frame size, many formulas have been developed to adjust saddle height. The most common formula bases the position on 109% of the measurement from your crotch to the floor in stocking feet. This measurement represents the distance between the pedal (with the crank parallel with the seat tube) and the top of the saddle (B, **Figure 14**).

The saddle can be positioned closer to or farther away from the handlebars (**Figure 15**). For leisurely touring, position the saddle nose 2-3 in. (5-8 mm) behind the bottom bracket center; move it closer for more spirited cycling. Measure the distance by dropping a plumb line from each point to the floor.

HANDLEBAR POSITION

There are 3 adjustments to make the handlebars fit you:
a. Height of the bars.
b. Longitudinal position.
c. Angle.

Correct positioning of the handlebars is a trial-and-error matter. As a rough guide, the top of the handlebars should be level with the seat. In addition, the measurement from the nose of the saddle to the rear edge of the top bar should equal the length of your arm from elbow to fingertips (**Figure 16**). Finally, the angle of the bottom of the bars on drop bars should be 10-15° with respect to the ground (**Figure 17**). These guidelines are rough and depend on your own body dimensions. Experiment with all 3 adjustments until the bike is comfortable for you.

The stem can be moved up and down to vary handlebar height. However, be sure that *at least* 2 1/2 in. (75 mm) of stem are in the head tube. If necessary, buy a longer stem.

Longitudinal adjustments are usually made by changing to a stem with a longer extension. Adjustable stems are available for some bikes.

BRAKE LEVER POSITION

Brake levers should be positioned for fast easy braking. If the bars are taped, remove the tape and reposition the brake levers on the curved portion of drop bars where they are easy to grab in an emergency. Retape the bars as described in Chapter Seven.

CHAPTER ELEVEN

ACCESSORIES, CLOTHING AND
SAFETY EQUIPMENT

The range of accessories, clothing and safety equipment available today is fantastic. Walk around in a fairly large bicycle dealership and you will see just about anything you could either add to the bicycle or want to wear. If you are going to do some serious cycling, don't forget the basic safety items such as a helmet, gloves, etc. Bicycles can be equipped with racks and pannier bags to personal belongings and equipment for long camping trips. Watch out for gimmick items that only add unnecessary weight.

The accessories, clothing and safety equipment listed in this chapter are the most commonly used. For every item shown in this chapter there are probably 10 similar items in a fairly large bicycle dealership. When you have decided on what type of goodies you want, go in and talk with a salesperson at a reputable bicycle dealership. They should steer you toward the right items for your specific needs. Watch out, though, as there is a fairly good profit margin in this type of gear—don't let them talk you into something that you don't want or need. Just like the bicycle you purchased, there is a considerable price range to choose from. You do get what you pay for, but some things are really overpriced.

ACCESSORIES

Lights

Front and rear lights are absolutely essential if you do any night cycling. They help you see where you are going and, most importantly, they let motorists and other cyclist see you.

Bicycle lights fall into 2 broad categories:
a. Generator-powered.
b. Battery-powered.

The generator-powered systems are quite reliable. The knurled wheel on the generator contacts the front or rear tire sidewall (**Figure 1**). One generator powers both front and rear lights. A generator comes in a kit (**Figure 2**) with all of the necessary items and instructions for installation. For best results, follow the manufacturer's instructions closely.

There are 2 major disadvantages. The generator requires added pedaling effort and the lights are on only while moving. When you stop moving you will be without lights.

Front and rear battery-powered lights usually have their own separate batteries. Most use 2 "D" cell batteries. The lights are completely self-contained and are simply clamped to the bicycle frame according to the manufacturer's directions.

11

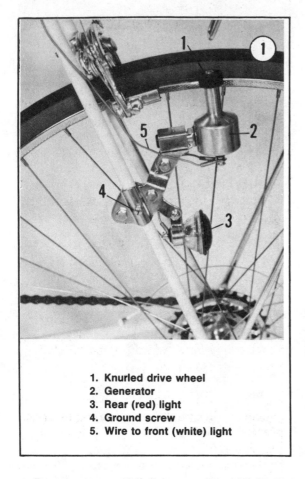

1. Knurled drive wheel
2. Generator
3. Rear (red) light
4. Ground screw
5. Wire to front (white) light

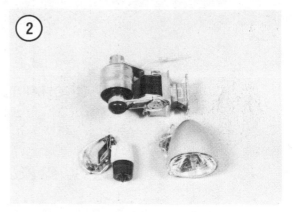

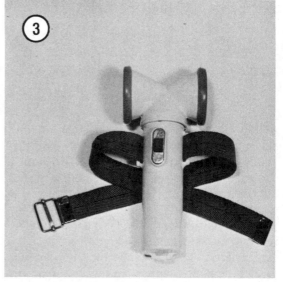

Battery-powered lights are not as reliable as generator lights due to battery failure. For best results and long life use a good quality alkaline battery (such as Duracell, Energizer, etc.). If you choose to buy battery-powered lights you may also want to invest in rechargable batteries and a battery recharger. It may pay for itself in the long run if you do a lot of night cycling mainly around your house (there is no place to plug in a recharger at that beautiful campsite in the woods). Battery-powered lights do not add to pedaling effort and the lights remain lighted when you are stopped (as long as the batteries are alive).

There are also lights (**Figure 3**) that can be strapped to your left arm or leg (the side toward traffic). This light provides a white light forward and a red light to the rear. When strapped to your leg, the light bobs up and down, adding to visibility. This light should be used in addition to bicycle-mounted electrical lights.

Troubleshooting
Generator-powered Lights

1. *Neither light comes on*—Usually caused by a faulty ground (tighten the ground screw), loose or dirty connections or a defective generator. It is also possible that both bulbs are loose or burned out. See the following symptoms.

2. *One light works, the other does not*—If one light works, the generator is operating and the ground must be all right. Check that mounting bolts for the defective light are not loose. Remove the bulb and look at filament inside. Replace the bulb if burned out. If bulb is good, lightly clean the metal end of the bulb with fine crocus cloth. Place a piece of crocus cloth over the end of a pencil and clean the

④

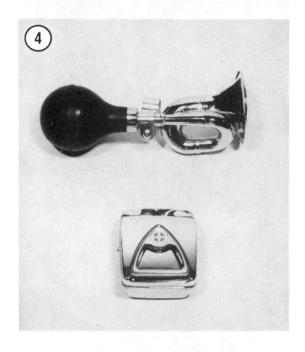

⑤

⑥

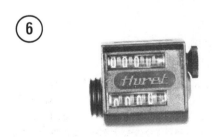

generator ground screw. If only one light is affected, check it as described in Step 2.

Reflectors

Most bicycles sold in the U.S. have reflectors installed as standard equipment. If you own a model without reflectors, they should be added. There should be the following reflex reflectors on the bicycle:
a. Front—white color.
b. Rear—red color.
c. Side (mounted on wheel spokes)—white or amber.

NOTE
When mounting reflectors on the wheel, mount them opposite the tire valve stem. This will help keep the wheel in balance.

Reflectors help drivers see you; they should be used *in addition to*, not instead of, electric lights.

Horns

There are 3 types of horns used on bicycles:
a. Squeeze bulb.
b. Electrical.
c. Freon boat horn.
Squeeze bulb horns and electrically powered bicycle horns (**Figure 4**) are little more than toys. They are not loud enough to warn motorists or pedestrians. Freon-powered boat horns are certainly loud enough to warn anyone, but a motorist is likely to misinterpret the noise; you may get run over by a motorist avoiding an imaginary truck. Any effort expended honking a horn may be better spent taking evasive action. If you must vent your anger, try hollering; it's more satisfying than a horn anyway.

Odometers and Speedometers

Several odometers and combination odometer/speedometers are available (**Figure 5**). Odometers fit on the front fork and are available for different size wheels (**Figure 6**). Combination odometer/speedometers usually connect to the front wheel via a cable. They are rarely as reliable as separate odometers and add additional weight.

11

contacts in the light housing as well. Check the electrical connections to the light housing. Disconnect it and clean the connection and lug on the end of the wire using crocus cloth. 3. *One or both lights very dim or flash erratically*—Normally caused by dirty electrical connections to light housing, faulty generator ground or faulty light housing grounds. If both lights are affected, tighten

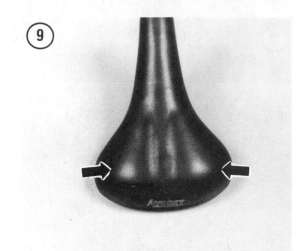

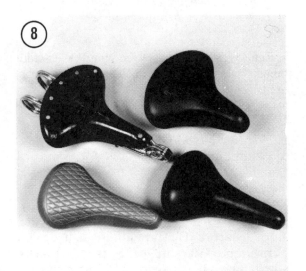

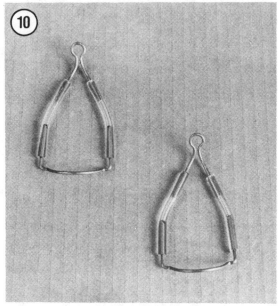

Bicycle Computer

Yes, that's right, your very own computer (**Figure 7**) right on the handlebar. These computers vary in price with the number of features they offer. Some of the basic ones give you a reading on speed, trip miles and elapsed time. Some of the more exotic ones will tell you distance, time, speed, average speed, maximum speed and also work as an odometer. There are also models that will give a heart rate reading from a belt that is worn around the chest or with sensors mounted on the handlebar grips.

Seats

There are a variety of aftermarket seats (**Figure 8**) available today. If you are not happy with the seat on your present bicycle, it is easy to replace.

The serious cyclist should consider one of the anatomically designed seats. This type of seat features 2 raised pads (**Figure 9**). The pads are located at the rear of the seat at the point where your pelvic bones make contact. Most brands offer one model for men and one for women as our posteriors are definitely different.

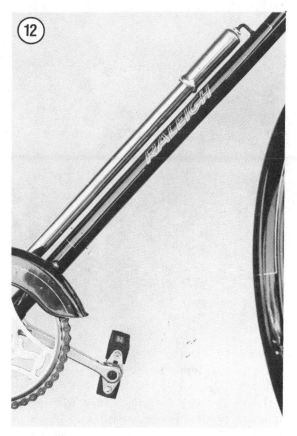

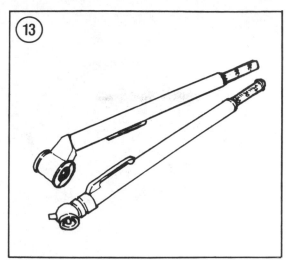

Tire Pumps

Large, efficient tire pumps (**Figure 11**) are made for home use. Smaller ones that mount on the bicycle (**Figure 12**) are made for road use. The pump must be fitted with a connection for Presta or Schraeder type valves as described in Chapter Four.

Be sure the pump will deliver enough air pressure for the tires on your bicycle. Some bicycle pumps are rated up to 200 psi but many automotive hand pumps will not deliver more than about 35 psi.

Tire Pressure Gauges

Improper tire inflation greatly affects handling and tire wear. Underinflation increases pedaling effort and tire wear. In addition, large bumps can seriously bruise the tire or damage the rim. Overinflation increases ride harshness and the likelihood of a tire blowout.

Several tire pressure gauges are available (**Figure 13**). Some have a dial face while others have a moving calibrated rod. Regardless of the type you prefer, be sure it is calibrated to at least 140 psi. Many gauges for automotive use do not register over 40-45 psi.

Control Cables

Aftermarket control cables (brake and derailleur) are available. These cables are usually of high quality material; some are covered to provide minimum friction within

Tire Savers
(Nail Pullers)

Tire savers (**Figure 10**) attach to the front and rear hand brake mounting post. They ride lightly on the tire and scrape away nails, glass or metal which may become embedded in the tire tread. They can be used only with smooth tread tubular tires.

11

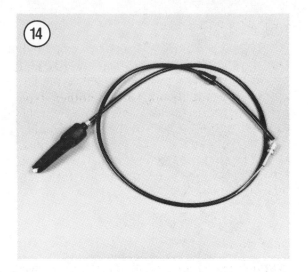

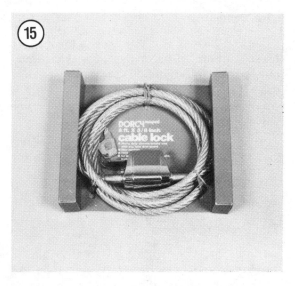

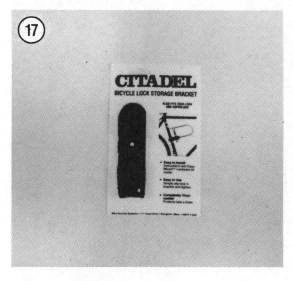

the cable sheath. Terrycable, a long-time motorcycle control cable manufacturer, makes such cables for BMX bicycles (**Figure 14**).

Locks

Choose a lock carefully. Unfortunately, you may need to carry a heavy lock and chain around to lock your expensive lightweight bicycle.

There are a variety of locking devices available today. These include a large case-hardened chain and padlock, a heavy-duty cable with an internal lock

(**Figure 15**) or the U-shaped, vinyl coated solid lock (**Figure 16**) with frame mounting bracket (**Figure 17**). The chain and cable can be covered with a vinyl tubing to prevent damage to the bicycle finish. Any chain or cable can be cut cleanly and quickly with bolt cutters.

Figure 18 shows how to lock your bicycle securely. If a tree or pole is nearby, loop the chain or cable through the frame, around the tree or pole and through both wheels. If using the U-shaped lock, you must lock the bicycle to a pole only. If nothing is available on which to chain the bicycle, loop the chain through the frame and through at least one wheel, preferably both. If you only have enough chain or cable to go through one wheel, lock the rear wheel as it is the most expensive. If you have quick release hubs, remove the front wheel, place it next to the rear wheel and lock them all together. Remember, this doesn't prevent someone from picking it up, lock, chain and all. It merely keeps honest people honest.

Auto Bicycle Carriers

Several types of bicycle carriers are offered. One type mounts on the rear bumper and carries 1 or 2 bicycles. There is one type that mounts on the trunk. Still another type permits several bicycles to be strapped on the car roof upside down. To fit the maximum number of bicycles on this type of rack, alternate them so every other one faces forward. Allow 14-16 in. width for each bicycle.

Baby Seats

Many baby seats are manufactured for use by children up to about 4 years old. Front-mounted seats make steering and balance difficult and very dangerous. Rear-mounted seats are perfectly safe, *provided* there are leg shields which protect the child's feet and legs from the wheel spokes (**Figure 19**). Other features to look for are adjustable footrests and a safety strap.

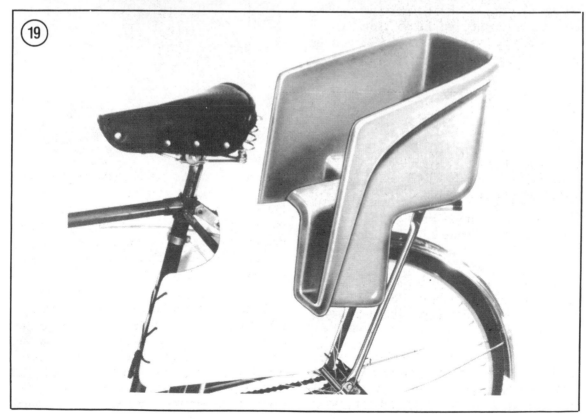

11

Racks and Packs

If you are going touring or even for a long day's ride you will want someplace to store extra clothes and edible goodies.

There are a variety of racks (**Figure 20**) that attach to the front and rear portion of the frame and axles. Then there are packs, called pannier bags, that attach to these racks or to the handlebar. These bags range from a simple handlebar pack to pannier bags that fit on each side of both the front and rear wheels.

Water Bottle

A metal or plastic water bottle that clips onto the frame (**Figure 21**) is almost a necessity for an all-day ride in hot weather. If you perspire a lot, you should also have a supply of salt tablets. These tablets taken with water will help keep the water from going right through your body.

CLOTHING

All types of cycling apparel is available for all age groups. Much of the exotic clothing comes from Europe but there is a lot available from the U.S. and the Orient. Just as with the other accessories listed in this chapter, some of the clothing is a must for the serious cyclist while other items are really unnecessary.

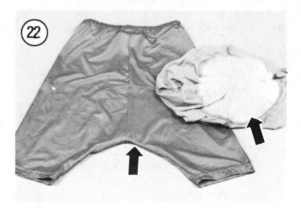

Shorts

One of the first items of clothing that you should purchase is a good pair of cycle shorts. These shorts are specially designed with a minimum of seams in the area where you sit. Most are also chamois lined on the inside of the crotch area (**Figure 22**). This helps reduce chafing and skin irritation.

Jersey

The jersey is no more than a special T-shirt. They do have 2 pockets (**Figure 23**) on the lower back to hold your wallet, etc. Some are cotton lined on the inside with a polyester layer on the outside.

There are many variations on jerseys; check them out at your nearest bicycle dealer.

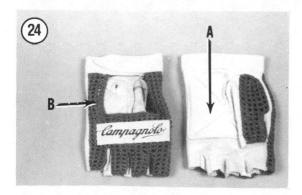

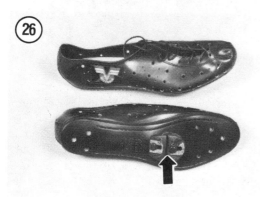

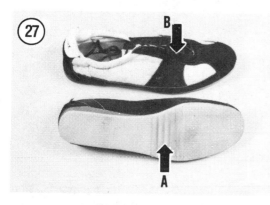

Gloves

Gloves are a necessity in cycling. There are many different types with various features and quite a price range. The main feature in a good glove is a padded palm (A, **Figure 24**). This pad absorbs a lot of the handlebar shock which helps minimize numbness in the hand during long rides. The back (B, **Figure 24**) should be 100% cotton to absorb hand moisture.

There are also special gloves for BMX racing (**Figure 25**). They do not have padded palms in order to "get the feel" of the bike during the race. Some are for wet weather racing.

Shoes

Special cycling shoes will help you pedal more easily and make cycling a lot more fun. The sole of the shoe where it makes contact with the pedal should be stiff. The stiff sole allows the leg force to transfer directly to the pedal without making the foot do a lot of unnecessary work. They are made out of lightweight material; the body may have holes for ventilation.

There are basically 2 different types of cycle shoes. One is strictly for cycling; the sole is so stiff that it will not bend. It is also fitted with a lug (**Figure 26**) that grips the pedal at the correct place. Many pedals have a special receptacle that grips the shoe lug.

> *NOTE*
> *Add a drop of SAE30 engine oil to the screw threads prior to installing the lug onto the shoe sole. This will allow easy removal for adjustment.*

11

The other shoe looks like a typical sports shoe and can also be used for walking. It does have special features just for cycling. The sole has angled wedges (A, **Figure 27**) to help grip the pedals. The sole is reinforced with a stiff material from the wedges on back to the heel to help with pedaling effort. There are padded side patches (B, **Figure 27**) to help prevent strap pain from the pedals.

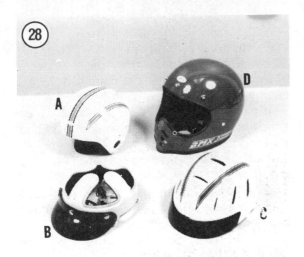

Cold Weather Items

There are many special items for cold weather and rainy weather riding. These include rain gear, lightweight parkas, even booties to go over your shoes to keep your feet warm. Check them out at a bicycle dealership.

SAFETY EQUIPMENT

Safety equipment is especially important if you do a lot of cycling in automobile traffic. Some of the items are not as comfortable as you would like them to be, but their safety value outweighs that inconvenience.

Helmet

The most important safety item is the helmet which should be worn at all times when cycling. There are various types of helmets to suit specific needs. A small child's helmet (A, **Figure 28**) protects a child when riding in a child seat or when riding on their own. There is the Skidlid (B, **Figure 28**), a semi-open type that offers protection plus good air circulation over the head. The typical helmet (C, **Figure 28**) has a visor to help keep the sun out of your eyes. For BMX racing you should use a full-face motorcycle type helmet (D, **Figure 28**) that also protects the face and jaw area.

The majority of these helmets will make your head warm, even with vents, but the protection they afford makes them a

necessity. The old motorcycle saying, "If you have a $10 head, wear a $10 helmet" applies equally to bicycling.

Rear View Mirrors

These could be considered an accessory but they are really a piece of safety equipment. There are 2 basic types of rear view mirrors—handlebar mounted and a clip-on type for the helmet or eyeglasses.

The handlebar type (**Figure 29**) attaches to the control cable portion of the hand caliper brake lever on the left-hand side. This type does vibrate with the handlebar.

The clip-on type (**Figure 30**) can be clipped onto the helmet or onto your eyeglasses. This

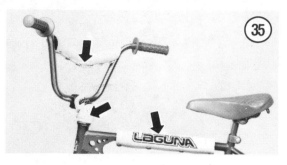

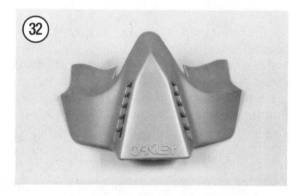

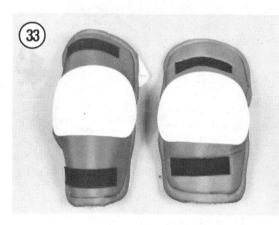

type does not vibrate and moves along with your head so you can always see what is behind you.

BMX Racing Equipment

The following items are suited mainly for BMX competition and practice. Some could also be used for everyday cycling if you so desire.

1. Helmet (D, **Figure 28**)—full face is the best for full protection.
2. Goggles (**Figure 31**)—should be worn with a helmet.
3. Face mask (**Figure 32**)—should be worn if a full-face helmet is not worn. This helps to protect the nose, mouth and jaw.
4. Knee pads (**Figure 33**)—good for protection of the knees. They are padded and are held in place by Velcro straps.
5. Elbow and forearm pads—wear to protect your arms in a spill. These are padded and are held in place with Velcro straps.
6. Chest protector—molded plastic perforated vest that protects the chest, collarbones and the shoulders.
7. Gloves (**Figure 25**)—to protect your hands and to get a better hold on the grips.
8. Pants and jerseys—added protection for the legs and upper body. They are usually made of a bonded fabric that is cool as well as protective.
9. Grips (**Figure 34**)—come in various configurations and softness.
10. Bike pads (**Figure 35**)—foam filled, vinyl covered pads that snap into place on the handlebar cross bar, stem and frame top tube. These pads will help take some of the pain out of a hard fall onto one of these components. They just may save your front teeth if you forget your face mask.

11

CHAPTER TWELVE

GEARING

DERAILLEUR GEAR RATIOS

Gear ratios for derailleur bicycles are not complicated, although the average person pays little attention to the choice of gears on a bicycle. Manufacturers choose widely spaced gear ratios for most bicycles. This enables the average person to select the proper gear for a wide variety of situations. Expensive bicycles often have closer spaced gear ratios for more specialized situations.

Bicycle gear ratios quoted by the manufacturer are determined by the ratio of rear sprocket teeth to front sprocket teeth, multiplied by the diameter of the wheel. For example, suppose a bicycle has 27 in. wheels, a 45 tooth front sprocket and a 15 tooth rear sprocket. The ratio of the sprockets is 3 (45 divided by 15). Multiply 3 by 27 (wheel diameter); the result is the gear ratio quoted by the manufacturer—81 gear. With one revolution of the crank, this bicycle covers the same distance as an old-fashioned high wheeler with an 81 in. diameter wheel.

It's easy to compute the actual distance covered for one turn of the crank on any bicycle. First, calculate the gear ratio for the sprockets and wheel, then multiply the result by pi (3.1417). In the example above, multiply 81 by 3.1417; the bicycle travels 254 in., approximately 21 ft.

Table 1 and **Table 2** simplify gear ratio computations. Refer to the table matching your wheel diameter. Find the column corresponding to the number of teeth on the rear sprocket. If you follow the 45 tooth column down to the 15 tooth row, you will see the number 81. Note that this is the same number calculated earlier.

For wheel sizes and sprockets not covered in the tables, use the following formula:

Number of front sprocket teeth divided by number of teeth on rear sprocket times wheel diameter = gear.

CADENCE

Experienced cyclists develop a rhythm and pedal at a relatively constant rate. This is called *cadence* and is measured in crank revolutions per minute. Each individual has his or her own natural cadence which feels most comfortable. For most amateur cyclists, the rate is 55-75 rpm; professional racers establish a cadence of over 100 rpm.

The gears on your bicycle permit you to maintain your most efficient, natural cadence regardless of conditions. When pedaling becomes too difficult to maintain a cadence, downshift. When it is too easy to pedal and there is little pedal resistance, upshift.

Figure 1 permits you to estimate your speed in miles per hour from your cadence. Since your cadence shouldn't vary much, you can memorize the figures for the gears you use most. To use the graph, find the gear ratio in use on the vertical scale. Follow it over to the desired cadence and read the speed directly below.

The dotted line in **Figure 1** shows an example. Suppose you are pedaling in 100 gear at 60 rpm; follow the 100 to the right until it touches the 60 line. Follow this point down to read your speed—about 18 mph.

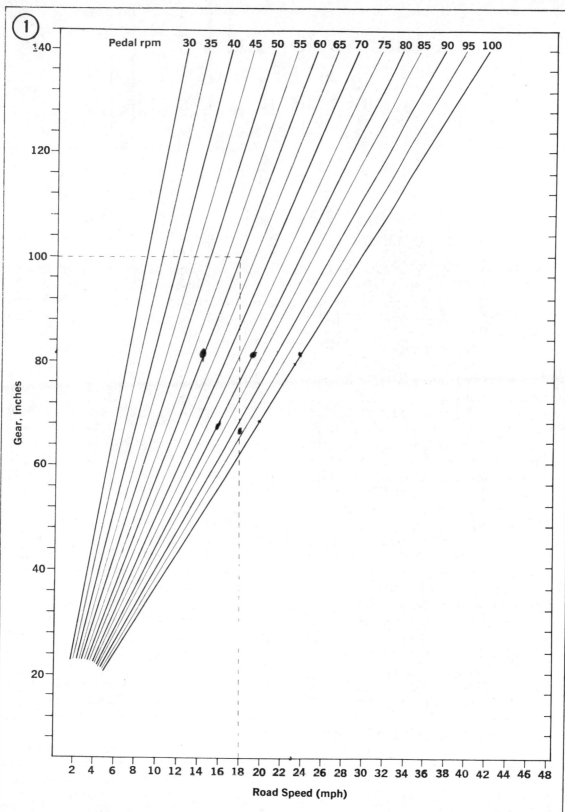

12

Table 1   26 INCH WHEEL

Teeth Per Rear Sprocket	Number of teeth, Chainwheel (large front sprocket)																					
	24	26	28	30	32	34	36	38	40	42	44	45	46	47	48	49	50	52	53	54	55	56
12	52.1	56.3	60.6	65.0	69.2	73.8	78.0	82.4	86.7	91.0	95.3	97.5	99.7	101.8	104.0	106.1	108.3	112.7	114.8	117.0	119.1	121.3
13	48.0	52.0	56.0	60.0	64.1	68.0	72.0	76.0	80.0	84.0	88.0	90.0	92.0	94.0	96.0	98.0	100.0	104.0	106.0	108.0	110.0	112.0
14	44.7	48.2	52.0	55.7	59.5	63.1	66.8	70.6	74.3	78.0	81.7	83.5	85.4	87.3	89.1	91.0	92.9	96.6	98.4	100.3	102.1	104.0
15	41.6	45.0	48.5	52.0	55.6	59.0	62.4	65.9	69.3	72.8	76.3	78.0	79.7	81.5	83.2	84.9	86.7	90.1	91.8	93.6	95.3	97.0
16	39.1	42.2	45.5	48.7	52.0	55.2	58.5	61.8	65.0	68.3	71.5	73.1	74.6	76.4	78.0	79.6	81.3	84.5	86.1	87.7	89.3	91.0
17	36.7	39.7	42.8	45.8	49.0	52.0	55.0	58.1	61.2	64.2	67.3	68.8	70.4	71.9	73.4	74.9	76.5	79.5	81.0	82.5	84.1	85.6
18	34.6	37.5	40.5	43.3	46.2	49.2	52.0	54.9	57.8	60.6	63.6	65.0	66.4	67.9	69.3	70.7	72.2	75.1	76.5	78.0	79.4	80.8
19	32.9	35.5	38.3	41.0	43.8	46.5	49.2	52.0	54.7	57.5	60.2	61.7	62.9	64.3	65.7	67.0	68.4	71.2	72.5	73.9	75.2	76.6
20	31.2	33.8	36.4	39.0	41.6	44.2	46.7	49.4	52.0	54.6	57.2	58.5	59.8	61.1	62.4	63.7	65.0	67.6	68.9	70.2	71.5	72.8
21	29.7	32.1	34.6	37.1	39.7	42.0	44.5	46.1	49.5	52.0	54.5	55.8	57.0	58.2	59.4	60.6	61.9	64.4	65.6	66.8	68.0	69.3
22	28.4	30.7	33.0	35.4	37.9	40.2	42.5	44.9	47.3	49.6	52.0	53.1	54.4	55.5	56.7	57.9	59.1	61.5	62.6	63.8	65.0	66.1
23	27.1	29.3	31.6	33.9	36.2	38.4	40.6	43.0	45.2	47.5	49.8	50.8	52.0	53.1	54.3	55.4	56.5	58.8	59.9	61.0	62.1	63.3
24	26.0	28.1	30.3	32.5	34.7	36.8	39.0	41.2	43.3	45.5	47.7	48.6	49.9	50.9	52.0	53.1	54.2	56.3	57.4	58.5	59.5	60.6
25	25.0	27.0	29.1	31.2	33.4	35.4	37.4	39.5	41.6	43.7	45.8	46.9	47.8	48.9	49.9	51.0	52.0	54.1	55.1	56.1	57.2	58.2
26	24.1	26.0	28.0	30.0	32.8	34.0	36.0	38.0	40.0	42.0	44.0	45.0	46.0	47.0	48.0	49.0	50.0	52.0	53.0	54.0	55.0	56.0
28	22.3	24.1	26.0	27.8	29.7	31.6	33.4	35.3	37.1	39.0	40.9	41.8	42.7	43.6	44.6	45.5	46.4	48.3	49.2	50.1	51.0	52.0

Table 2   GEAR RATIOS — 27 INCH WHEEL

Number of teeth, Chainwheel (large front sprocket)

Teeth Per Rear Sprocket	24	26	28	30	32	34	36	38	40	42	44	45	46	47	48	49	50	52	53	54	55	56
12	54.0	58.5	63.0	67.5	72.0	76.5	81.0	85.5	90.0	94.5	99.0	101.2	103.5	105.7	108.0	110.2	112.3	117.0	119.3	121.5	122.7	126.0
13	49.8	54.0	58.1	62.3	66.4	70.6	74.7	78.9	83.1	87.2	91.4	93.4	95.5	97.6	99.7	101.8	103.9	108.0	110.0	112.1	114.2	116.3
14	46.2	50.1	54.0	57.8	61.7	65.5	69.5	73.3	77.1	81.0	84.9	86.7	88.7	90.6	92.6	94.5	96.4	100.3	102.2	104.1	106.0	108.0
15	43.2	46.8	50.4	54.0	57.6	61.1	64.8	68.4	72.0	75.6	79.2	81.0	82.8	84.6	86.4	88.2	90.0	93.6	95.4	97.2	99.0	100.8
16	40.5	43.7	47.2	50.6	54.0	57.2	60.9	64.1	67.5	70.9	74.3	76.0	77.6	79.3	81.0	82.7	84.4	87.8	89.4	91.1	92.8	94.5
17	38.1	41.2	44.4	47.6	50.8	54.0	57.2	60.3	63.5	66.7	69.9	71.5	73.1	74.6	76.2	77.8	79.4	82.6	84.1	85.7	87.3	88.9
18	36.0	39.0	42.0	45.0	48.0	51.0	54.0	57.0	60.0	63.0	66.0	67.5	69.0	70.5	72.0	73.5	75.0	78.0	79.5	81.0	82.5	84.0
19	34.1	36.8	39.7	42.6	45.5	48.2	51.1	54.0	56.8	59.7	62.5	64.0	65.4	66.8	68.2	69.6	71.1	73.9	75.3	76.7	78.1	79.5
20	32.4	35.1	37.8	40.5	43.2	45.9	48.7	51.3	54.0	56.7	59.4	60.8	62.1	63.4	64.8	66.2	67.5	70.2	71.5	72.9	74.5	75.6
21	30.8	33.4	36.0	38.6	41.1	43.7	46.4	48.9	51.4	54.0	56.6	57.9	59.1	60.4	61.7	63.0	64.3	66.9	68.1	69.4	70.7	72.0
22	29.4	31.9	34.3	36.8	39.2	41.6	44.2	46.6	49.1	51.5	54.0	55.2	56.5	57.6	58.9	60.1	61.4	63.8	65.0	66.2	67.5	68.7
23	28.1	30.5	32.8	35.2	37.5	39.9	42.4	44.6	47.0	49.3	51.6	52.8	54.0	55.2	56.3	57.5	58.7	61.0	62.2	63.6	64.5	65.7
24	27.0	29.2	31.5	33.7	36.0	38.2	40.5	42.8	45.0	47.3	49.5	50.7	51.8	52.9	54.0	55.1	56.3	58.6	59.6	60.7	61.8	63.0
25	25.9	28.0	30.2	32.4	34.6	36.7	38.9	41.0	43.2	45.4	47.5	48.6	49.7	50.8	51.8	52.9	54.0	56.2	57.2	58.3	59.4	60.4
26	24.9	27.0	29.0	31.2	33.2	35.3	37.4	39.5	41.5	43.6	45.7	46.7	47.8	48.8	49.9	50.9	51.9	54.0	55.0	56.0	57.1	58.1
27	24.0	26.0	28.0	30.0	32.0	34.0	36.0	38.0	40.0	42.0	44.0	45.0	46.0	47.0	480	49.0	50.0	52.0	53.0	54.0	55.0	56.0
28	23.1	25.0	27.0	28.9	30.8	32.8	34.8	36.6	38.6	40.5	42.4	43.4	44.4	45.3	46.3	47.2	48.2	50.1	51.1	52.0	53.0	54.0

12

CHAPTER THIRTEEN

RIDING SAFELY

This chapter explains the basics of riding a bicycle safely and correctly. Bicycle riding can be a lot of fun and will help keep you in good physical condition. It is a lot less monotonous than jogging and many doctors say it is better for you, as it puts less strain on some parts of your body.

Along with the fun of bicycling comes the risk of serious injuries and even death. The age group with the highest injury rate is the 10-14 year old group followed by the 5-9 year olds. After you reach 20 years your chances of injury drop off drastically. But look out after you reach 64, because after that the injury rate starts to climb again.

The injury rate is especially high when riding in areas with heavy automobile traffic. When a bicycle and an automobile come together in an accident, the bicycle and bicycle rider always lose. Be extra careful when riding in traffic. Automobiles drivers have a difficult time seeing motorcycles stopped at traffic signals or boulevard stop signs; imagine how much more difficult it is to see a bicycle with a small rider.

BASIC SAFETY RULES

1. Make sure that your brakes work correctly. Being able to stop quickly may avoid an accident and save your life. Prior to each ride, test the brakes and adjust them if necessary.
2. Make sure the handlebar is tightly secured to the stem (**Figure 1**) and front fork and that the saddle is secured in the seat tube (**Figure 2**). Make sure that both wheel axles are tight as shown in **Figure 3** and **Figure 4**. Make sure that both tires are inflated to the proper pressure. Refer to the inflation pressure tables in Chapter Three. Check these items prior to each ride.

3. Obey all traffic regulations governing automobiles in your local area. After all, you are sharing the same roadway.

4. Keep to the right-hand side of the roadway going in the same direction as traffic. If riding in a group, ride single file on the right-hand side of the road. Watch out for parked cars; the driver's side door(s) may open or the car may pull out into traffic. Be prepared to stop.

5. Avoid riding on the sidewalks. If local ordinances allow sidewalk riding, give

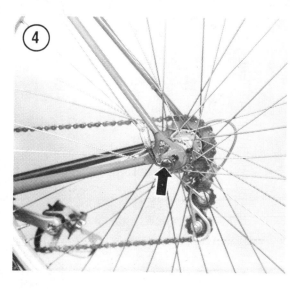

pedestrains the right-of-way. A bicycle rider makes very little noise—do not come up behind a pedestrian and startle them with a horn, bell or shout.

6. Don't take shortcuts over lawns or through private property.

7. On multi-speed bicycles, be sure to shift into a middle gear prior to coming to a stop. This way you will be in the correct gear for starting out in traffic.

8. Have some sort of warning device on the bicycle—a horn, a bell or similar device to warn other people that you are approaching.

9. Do not carry another passenger on your bicycle unless it is a tandem bicycle or is equipped with a child's seat. In many areas it is illegal to ride 2 people on a bicycle designed for the rider only.

10. Use arm signals when making turns so that automobile drivers as well as other bicyclists are aware of what you are planning to do next:

    a. Left-hand turn—left arm extended straight out to the left and horizontal to the ground.

    b. Right-hand turn—left arm extended to the left with the elbow bent and the forearm straight up.

    c. Slow down or stop—left arm extended to the left with the forearm bent at the elbow straight down.

11. Always keep both hands on the handlebar except when signaling for turns. This way you can maintain control of the bicycle.

12. Don't fool around on the bicycle in traffic. Doing so will probably lead to an accident resulting in an injury. Never hold onto a car, moped or motorcycle that is moving. Stay away from "Look, Ma, no hands" tricks; you may end up with them injured.

13. Do not carry packages in your hands or under your arms. Install a carrier, a rack or a basket for packages. You need both hands on the handlebar to maintain control of the bicycle. There should also be an unobstructed view all around you.

14. When entering an intersection, look both ways several times.

13

15. Bicycle lights are very important at night. The bicycle should be equipped with a white light on the front and red light on the rear.

16. Wear a safety helmet when riding; this also goes for a small child that may be riding in a child's seat.

17. When riding at night you should wear light colored clothing, preferably white. Apply some strips of reflective tape to your riding clothes and helmet for added safety.

18. Use a rear view mirror. These mirrors can be mounted on the handlebar, your helmet or your eyeglasses.

19. Most bicycles manufactured today are equipped with a white reflex reflector on the front, a red one on the rear and either an amber or white reflector attached to the spokes of each wheel. If your bicycle is not equipped this way or they have been removed, install new ones.

20. Be careful when looking over your shoulder. Most riders will drift toward the right when looking over their left-hand shoulder and will drift to the left when looking over their right-hand shoulder.

21. When you stop your bicycle for a rest be courteous to other people in the area:
   a. Don't park your bicycle near a door leading into a business establishment.
   b. Move your bicycle off the roadway.
   c. Don't lean your bicycle against a large plate glass window.
   d. Be courteous to other people that may come by while you are resting.

LEARNING TO RIDE

Learning to ride a lightweight multi-speed bicycle is not as easy as it may sound. Today's lightweight bicycles are different from the older heavy single-speed ones many of us grew up on. The lightweights travel at a much higher rate of speed and handle much better. It's like jumping out of the family sedan into a sports car. You must be a lot quicker and more alert or you may find yourself in trouble.

Do not get on your new 10-speed and try to learn how to shift gears, maintain your balance and perform 2-wheel braking on the street in front of your house. You don't want

all of your neighbors see you take your first spill anyway.

Try to find a local bicycle club. Check with bicycle shops for any local bicycle clubs. If you are lucky enough to have one close by, contact them as they may have a class for beginning cyclists or at least there may be someone who can coach you on the basics of good riding. This is really the best way to learn.

If there are no local clubs, take the bicycle to a quiet secluded area where there is little or no traffic. Use a local business's parking lot on a weekend (when there are no cars parked). Find one that is level and has a relatively smooth surface with as few cracks and bumps as possible. If a parking lot is not available, find a lightly-traveled street that has no potholes. Use the information in the following paragraphs on how to become acquainted and proficient on your new lightweight multi-speed bicycle. Remember that there is no substitute for practice, practice, practice. Don't plan a 50-100 mile trip right after purchasing your new bicycle. Take your time not only to get used to the bicycle and build up your cycling skills but also to get your body in shape for a long ride. You will have plenty of sore muscles after the first ride on your new bicycle.

The following riding suggestions assume that you already know how to ride a bicycle, whether it was as a child or on an old heavy single speed.

Adjusting All Components

Prior to starting on your first ride make sure that the bicycle is set up correctly for you. This will make riding a lot more pleasant and safe. Adjust the handlebar, saddle, brake levers, etc. as described in Chapter Ten.

Selecting The Proper Gear
For Getting Underway

You can get underway with the bicycle in any gear but if the gear ratios are either very high or very low it may be difficult. The best gear in which to start is one of the middle gears. After you have been riding for a time you will automatically shift down into a lower gear when you are coming to a stop.

CAUTION

In order to shift gears correctly the pedals, chain and rear wheel must be rotating forward or the derailleur(s) will be damaged. Never try to shift gears without all of these components in motion.

If your bicycle is not positioned into one of the middle gears perform the following:

a. Place a blanket on the ground to protect the saddle and handlebar.

b. Turn the bicycle upside down on the blanket so the bicycle is resting on the saddle and the handlebar.

c. Rotate the pedals by hand in the correct direction and make sure the rear wheel is turning forward.

d. Gently move the shifter for the rear derailleur until the drive chain moves to the second largest rear sprocket.

e. Make sure the derailleur has correctly positioned the chain so it is not rubbing on the sprocket on either side of the second largest sprocket. *Slightly* move shifter in either direction until the chain runs smoothly and easily with no rubbing noise.

NOTE

The following steps are necessary if your bicycle has 10 speeds or more. A 5-speed bicycle has only one front chainwheel.

f. Again rotate the pedals by hand in the correct direction and make sure the rear wheel is turning forward.

g. Gently move the shifter for the front derailleur until the drive chain moves to the largest or outside chainwheel.

h. Make sure the derailleur has correctly positioned the chain so it is not rubbing on the side of the derailleur guide. *Slightly* move the shifter in either direction until the guide moves away from the chain so there is no rubbing noise.

i. The chain is now positioned into the middle gear.

j. Turn the bicycle over onto its wheels. You are now ready to ride.

Mounting and Dismounting The Bicycle

Forget about the old way of placing one foot on a pedal, pushing the bicycle along and then throwing the other leg up and over the saddle. This method is too unstable for lightweight bicycles. The following method is suggested:

a. The bicycle must be in a middle gear.

b. With the bicycle stationary and one of the hand brakes applied, raise one leg up and over the saddle (or through the frame opening on a woman's frame) and straddle the frame. Place both feet on the ground.

c. Position one pedal in the forward position at about 45° up from horizontal. This will be called the power stroke pedal.

d. Keep one foot on the ground and place the other foot on the power stoke pedal.

e. Push down on the power stroke pedal with your leg and the bicycle will start moving forward. Place the other foot on the other pedal, continue to pedal and slide back onto the saddle. You are now under way; ride around your practice area. Don't try to shift gears now, just ride around and enjoy yourself. Shifting gears will come later after you are more proficient at riding in a straight line and around in circles.

f. To stop and dismount, apply the brakes to slow down.

g. Place your weight on one pedal in the completely down position and slide off the saddle.

h. Move the other foot off the pedal and place it on the ground to support yourself as the bicycle comes to a complete stop.

i. Keep at least one of the brakes applied, raise one leg up and over the saddle (or through the frame) and dismount the bicycle.

Riding Position

Now that you are on the bicycle and it's moving forward you must be comfortable in order to enjoy your cycling.

13

1. For recreational riding, position your buttocks toward the rear or widest portion of the saddle.

2. Place your hands on the top portion of the handlebars on each side of the stem. Place them out as far as possible, just inboard of where the handlebar starts to bend forward.

3. Do not get a "strangle hold" on the handlebar as this will use up a lot of energy. Hold onto the handlebar with a relaxed grip. The bicycle is designed to travel in a straight line which means little effort is required to keep the handlebar in the straight-ahead position.

4. Keep your elbows slightly bent—do not lock them as this may put a strain on your arms and back. Also it is a lot safer to ride with the elbows slightly bent. If you are bumped from the side by another cyclist and your elbows are bent, the force will only move your arms. If your arms are locked, the bumping force will be transferred directly to the handlebar which may force the bicycle to move to one side.

5. By sitting on the saddle correctly and holding onto the handlebar correctly your weight will be evenly distributed. Your back will be positioned at less than 45° from true vertical. This is a good position for normal recreational cycling.

6. For more aggressive riding (to be used after you are more acquainted with the bicycle), move the hands farther outward on the handlebar until they are at the backside of the brake levers. At this point your back is positioned at greater than 45° from true vertical.

7. By bending farther forward and placing your hands on the lower loop of the handlebar you will gain even more power as well as cut down on wind resistance. The position of the back determines which muscles are used for pedaling effort. The most powerful muscle, the gluteus maximus, comes into use only when the back is at greater than 45° from a true vertical. By bending the elbows even further the back can be further lowered which will give you even more power.

Pedaling and Maintaining a Cadence

The correct foot-to-pedal placement is with the ball of the foot placed over the center of the pedal. This will give maximum pedal effectiveness and minimum foot and leg effort. Do not use the arch or heel of the foot. As you get more into cycling you will probably purchase a pair of cycle shoes. These shoes have a solid sole or have lugs on the sole that will automatically position your foot onto the pedal in this correct placement. These shoes are described in Chapter Eleven.

Try to maintain a good consistant cadence or same rate of pedal speed (not bicycle speed) at all times. This skill is something that should be learned right away as it makes cycling much easier. At first it requires a considerable amount of concentration but after awhile it becomes second nature. There is no specified cadence as that depends greatly on you, your bicycle and how fast or slow you want to travel. The important thing is a consistant pedal speed. Being able to maintain a good cadence will also help you handle gear shifting. The combination of these two techniques will enable you to get the most out of your bicycle.

When you first start riding and your legs begin to tire, slow down or stop and take a rest. It will take some time to become physically fit both in breathing and muscle stamina to go for long rides or to take on a hill. Don't try to do too much all at once as it will lead to frustration and a sore body.

Gear Shifting

Using the gears on a multi-speed bicycle correctly is one of the most difficult tasks to master. A novice rider should stay away from shifting gears until they have mastered the rest of the bicycle.

There are 3 major things that you must know about shifting gears with a derailleur mechanism.

1. In order to shift gears correctly the pedals, chain and rear wheel must be rotating forward or the derailleur(s) will be damaged. Do not shift gears while pedaling hard (such as up a hill). If you must shift gears while going up a hill, decrease your pedaling

cadence so you are *not* actually propelling the bicycle forward. All of the previously mentioned components should be rotating but there should be no load on them.

2. For a major gear ratio change, use the front derailleur and change the chain position on the front chainwheel. For minor gear ratio changes, use the rear derailleur and change the chain position on the rear sprockets.

3. There is no exact location of the shifter to indicate what gear you are in. The cables that actuate the derailleurs stretch with use so the lever will never be in the same exact position twice.

On *most* modern multi-speed bicycles, the left-hand shift lever controls the front chainwheels and the right-hand shift lever controls the rear sprocket gears. The shifters are usually located on the frame down tube or on a bracket adjacent to the stem.

To learn to change gears:

1. Take the bicycle to a quiet secluded area where there is little or no traffic. Use a local business's parking lot on a weekend (when there are no cars parked). Find one that is level and has a relatively smooth surface with as few cracks and bumps as possible. If a parking lot is not available, find a lightly-traveled street that has no potholes.

2. Get the bicycle moving forward at a moderate speed.

CAUTION
When you are changing gears and the chain gets caught or stuck, **stop immediately**. *Locate and correct the prblem. Never try to "fix" a problem by pedaling harder. Chances are you will only make the problem worse.*

3. Gently move the shifter that controls the front derailleur and change gears. There will be a lot of rattling and weird noises as the chain is moved from one sprocket to the other on the chainwheel. After the gear change is completed there should be no noise or scraping sounds coming from the derailleur guide. Make sure the derailleur has correctly positioned the chain so it is not rubbing on either side of the deraillcur guide. *Slightly* move the shifter in the opposite direction from which it was originally moved until the

guide moves away from the chain. There must be no rubbing noise. This minor adjustment is necessary; otherwise, the guide will wear prematurely or it may bend and eventually break. If the chain was moved from the small sprocket to the large sprocket, pedaling effort should greatly increase. If the chain was moved from the large sprocket to the small sprocket, pedaling effort should greatly decrease.

4. Gently move the shifter that controls the rear derailleur and change gears. The rear lever will travel a shorter amount to change the chain from one sprocket to another. Move it more slowly so you will change only one gear at a time. Again there will be some noise but not as much as with the front derailleur. After the gear change is completed there should be no noise from the derailleur. Make sure the derailleur has correctly positioned the chain so it is not rubbing on the side of one of the other sprockets. *Slightly* move the shifter in either direction until there is no rubbing noise.

NOTE
Practice changing gears with the rear derailleur so that you are proficient at changing only one gear at a time while maintaining the same pedal cadence.

5. One good rule-of-thumb in selecting the correct gear for the terrain in which you are riding is that if you have selected too high of a gear your legs will tire before your lungs will. If you have selected too low a gear your lungs will tire before your legs will. A high gear is one that requires a lot of pressure on the pedals. A low gear is one that requires relatively little pressure on the pedals.

Riding In A Straight Line

Being able to ride in a straight line without swerving is a tremendous skill that every cyclist should have. If you are able to do this, you will be more at ease when riding in heavy automotive traffic. You should be able to accelerate, shift gears and brake all within a straight line.

The only way to learn this skill is to practice it over and over again in a vacant parking lot or quiet roadway. Try to find an

13

area where there are some painted straight lines that you can ride on. Begin from a standing start, pedal and shift gears several times then brake to a stop all within the width of a painted line. Repeat this many times until you feel very comfortable doing it.

When you feel comfortable with your ability, perform the same series of events close to the side of the roadway or next to a curb. Riding next to the curb is very important as that is where most of your city riding will be done. Also, most designated bicycle paths are located next to a curb.

After you feel you have mastered this skill have some friends, who have also mastered the skill, practice the routines in a group formation in single file. Leave about 2 to 3 feet between your front wheel and the rear wheel of the bicycle ahead of you. Try changing speeds, maneuvering in and out and simulating situations that you would encounter when riding in a group in traffic on a roadway.

One-hand Riding

There are times when it is necessary to remove one of your hands from the handlebar. It is necessary when shifting gears, signaling for a turn or wiping the sweat off of the end of your nose. If this routine is not handled properly it can result in loss of control of the bicycle.

Move the hand that is to be left on the handlebar to the center of the handlebar, next to the stem. This will distribute your weight evenly on the handlebar and the front of the bicycle. Support your body weight with your stomach and back muscles prior to removing the other hand from the handlebar. With the fixed hand in this position you can then remove the other hand from the handlebar to do whatever must be done.

Do not ride in this position any longer than necessary as you do not have the same amount of control as with both hands on the handlebar.

Avoiding Road Obstacles

Learning to avoid obstacles on the roadway while maintaining control of the bicycle is a must. There is no telling what you will come across on the road, not to mention what someone may toss out of a car window ahead of you. Once again, use a deserted street or parking lot and set up a slalom course with empty aluminum beverage cans. That way if you happen to hit one it will cause litte or no damage to the bicycle or tire. Ride around them trying to avoid hitting any of them. As you get better at it, move the cans closer and closer together and change the course frequently.

Using The Brakes

From the very beginning you should learn to use both front and rear brakes at the same time. Apply the brakes gently at first until you become accustomed to how they operate. *Do not* apply the front brake only as you will end up going over the handlebar.

The stopping ability of your bicycle depends on some of the following factors:

a. Your reaction time.

b. The speed at which you are traveling.

c. Condition and adustment of the brakes on the bicycle.

d. Condition of the roadway (gravel, wet, icy, etc.).

You should practice straight line braking on a level surface at first. After you feel comfortable with straight line braking, try braking while making a turn. This one can be tricky; you may lose steering control at first. This type of braking must be practiced again and again as you must be proficient at it to ride safely in traffic.

After getting the feel for braking in a straight line and while turning you should run some brake tests on yourself. These tests can be run with other cyclists but do it on your own until you feel confident. Wear protective clothing and a helmet. Pick an area that is open, preferably flat and smooth. Mark a starting line and within about 200 ft. (61 m) mark a stopping line. You will need an assistant with a stop watch. Start pedaling from the start line and pedal as fast as you can. Slow down and come to a complete stop at the stop line. Have your assistant time you for the total elapsed time from start to finish. Write down the times for a comparison. Your best time will be when you can judge where

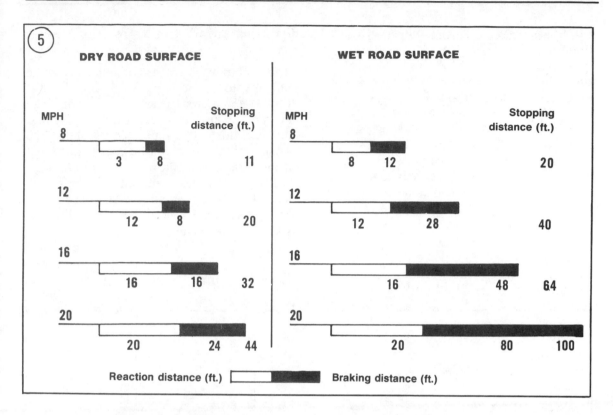

DRY ROAD SURFACE | WET ROAD SURFACE

MPH — Stopping distance (ft.)
MPH — Stopping distance (ft.)

Reaction distance (ft.) □ Braking distance (ft.) ▮

the stop line is, apply your brakes hard (avoid locking them up and don't go over the handlebar) and come to a complete stop on the line. Try different lever pressures to avoid locking up the brakes

If possible, simulate wet weather braking. Wet down the riding/braking area, the bicycle rims and the brake pads. This is not a true test but it will give you an idea of how less efficient the brakes are when wet. Repeat the dry run tests, record the times and compare the elapsed times. Also compare how many times you skidded on the wet pavement. Wipe down the bike and thoroughly dry off all components.

Downhill braking can also be tricky as the rider's weight is transferred toward the front even more so than when braking on the level. On downhill braking, bend down at the waist and transfer some of your body weight toward the rear by sliding back in the saddle. If the rear wheel starts to skid there is no way of predicting where the wheel is going to travel except toward the front of the bike. If the rear wheel starts to skid, let up on the brakes momentarily. This will help to straighten out

the bike. Then reapply the brake and complete your stop.

Brake very cautiously immediately after a rain or drizzle. The water will lift road oil and grease out of the pavement. The water and grease/oil combination will decrease brake effectiveness by about 50%.

Just as when braking in an automobile there is always the factor of reaction time. Reaction time is the time it takes the rider to first apply the brakes after recognizing the need to stop. The reaction time varies with individuals and also with the amount of rider concentration at the time. The average time is 3/4 of a second. That means that if you are traveling at 20 mph (32 km) you will travel a distance of 20 ft. (6 m) before you start to apply the brakes. After the brakes are applied, on dry, level pavement you will travel an additional 24 ft. (7 m) before coming to a complete stop. This equals a total distance of 44 ft. (13 m) traveled before coming to a complete stop. If stopping while going downhill the stopping distance greatly increases. Refer to **Figure 5** for examples of approximate reaction time and stopping

13

distances on dry, level ground with good brakes.

Hand operated caliper brakes must be maintained in good condition and adjusted correctly. As the brake pads wear the brake lever comes closer to the handlebar. If not adjusted periodically the brake lever will come in contact with the handlebar before full braking ability is achieved. The brake cables must also be lubricated routinely to minimize the amount of pressure required to properly apply the brakes. Refer to Chapter Five for service procedures related to the brakes.

NOTE
Foot operated coaster brakes do not require routine adjustment.

Cornering And Making Turns

Taking on a turn when going slow is no problem but when you are traveling fast it is a different story. Cornering is not as difficult as it may seem at first. There is a "line" through a corner, or turn, that seems to work the best under almost all circumstances. This line consists of the entrance, the apex and the exit of the turn. If you can make a turn around a corner with the least amount of turning the handlebar the better off you are. The larger the radius around a turn the better and safer it is as shown in **Figure 6**.

The road condition is even more critical when cornering than during straight line riding. Any gravel, sand, wet pavement, oil,

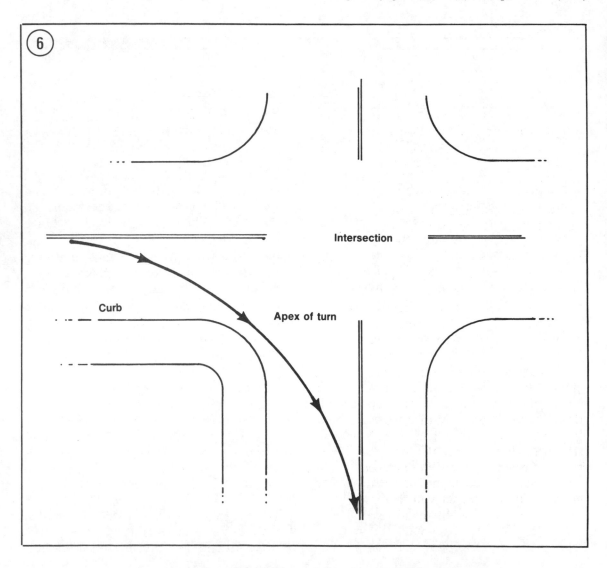

grease, wet leaves, ice, etc., will result in a spill if you are not very careful.

When taking on a corner you must contend with another evil called *centrifugal effect*. This is the effect of being pushed outward while negotiating a turn. Centrifugal effect is stronger when the bike is trying to make a tight turn. Therefore if you are traveling fast you should plan on a large radius for a safe turn. This will decrease the centrifugal effect on the bicycle. Watch out when negotiating a large turn in traffic; make sure that you do not go out so far that you meet oncoming traffic.

If you feel that you are traveling too fast for the oncoming turn, try to brake before entering the turn, not while you are cornering. If you must apply the brakes while cornering, apply the rear brakes first and then the front. If the front brakes are applied too hard at first, the front wheel will slide out from under you and you will go down. If you brake too hard with only the rear brakes, the rear end will try to slide out from under you. For safe cornering, brake before the turn, coast through the turn and pedal out of the turn.

When you pedal through a corner try to keep the bicycle in the most upright position possible. Keeping the bicycle upright will lessen the possibility of hitting the pedals on the roadway. An accident is sure to happen if the pedal strikes the roadway while pedaling through a corner. When going through a left-hand corner, move the upper body (from the waist up) toward the left and bend the elbows a little more than usual. This will place your nose almost directly over the left-hand side of the handlebar. For a right-hand turn, the opposite is true.

To coast through a corner, transfer your body weight from the seat (high center of gravity) to the pedals (low center of gravity). On a left-hand turn, move the upper body (from the waist up) toward the left and bend the elbows a little more than usual. Your nose should be directly over the left-hand side of the handlebar. Place the left-hand pedal in the *up* position and the right-hand pedal in the *down* position. Transfer your body weight to the outside pedal (right-hand) as this will lower the center of gravity. To make a right-hand turn, the opposite is true.

Making a left-hand turn in traffic can be terrifying. Even though it may be legal, do not make a left-hand turn from the left turn lane along with cars. It may take a little longer but it is a lot safer to use the following method:
1. Go through the intersection in the right-hand lane and come to a stop at the other side.
2. Back the bicycle around the corner.
3. When the traffic signal changes, proceed in the right-hand lane with the flow of traffic.

To make a right-hand turn after stopping at the intersection use the following method:
1. Come to a stop at the intersection. Stay back about 10 ft. (3 m) from the intersection.
2. Let the cars make their turn first when the light changes.
3. Make your turn but stay close to the curb as another car may sneak up behind you and also make a right-hand turn.

Road Hazards

Always be looking ahead for debris or hazards on the roadway such as broken glass, gravel, ruts, pot holes, railroad tracks and storm drain gratings. Try to look far enough ahead so there are few last-minute panics. Before swerving to the left to avoid something in the roadway, look back over your shoulder and make sure there are no automobiles directly behind you. If there is traffic, slow down and stop if possible. Avoid a panic stop as this may throw you out into traffic. If stopping is not possible, stand up on the pedals with your legs slightly bent at the knees. Hold onto the handlebar and coast through the debris, ruts, etc. Let your legs take most of the shock and not the bicycle.

When approaching railroad tracks always slow down and cross them at right angles or 90° to the tracks. If the tracks run across the roadway at a 45° angle be very careful that your tire does not get caught in the rail groove. It is almost impossible to steer out of the groove and you will lose steering control. Slow down and try to cross them at a right angle.

Watch out for running water on the roadway. You don't know how deep it is or if it may contain oil or other hidden debris. It

13

may also have mud at the bottom which will either slow you down drastically or stop you.

Look out for metal storm drain gratings on the roadway. If you get your wheel caught in the grating you will come to a complete stop instantly and fly up over the handlebars. The front wheel will also be damaged and maybe the fork. In trying to avoid a grating be sure to look over your shoulder and check for traffic. If you can't avoid the grating, stop the bike and walk it over or around the grating.

In warm weather, look out for tar patches. These will become quite slippery or sticky if the sun has been on them all day. Your front wheel may either slip to one side or get stuck in the tar and bring you to a complete stop. Avoid them if at all possible.

In general, always look ahead so that you have ample time to avoid any debris. Prior to moving to the left to avoid something, look over your shoulder and check for oncoming traffic.

INDEX

14

14

NOTES

NOTES

NOTES

Building Wheels   J - BRANDT